THE
SUMMER
OLYMPICS

GREAT MOMENTS IN THE

SUMMER OLYMPICS

By **MATT CHRISTOPHER**®

The #1 Sports Series for Kids

LITTLE, BROWN AND COMPANY
NEW YORK • BOSTON

Little, Brown and Company

Hachette Book Group
237 Park Avenue, New York, NY 10017
Visit our website at www.lb-kids.com

www.mattchristopher.com

Little, Brown and Company is a division of Hachette Book Group, Inc.
The Little, Brown name and logo are trademarks of Hachette Book Group, Inc.

The publisher is not responsible for websites (or their content)
that are not owned by the publisher.

First Edition: May 2012

Matt Christopher® is a registered trademark of Matt Christopher Royalties, Inc.

Text written by Stephanie True Peters

Library of Congress Cataloging-in-Publication Data

Christopher, Matt.
Great moments in the summer Olympics / Matt Christopher.
    p. cm. —(The #1 sports series for kids)
    ISBN 978-0-316-19579-9
    1. Olympics—History—Juvenile literature. I. Title.
    GV721.53.C47 2012
    796.48—dc23   2011026753

10 9 8 7 6 5 4 3 2 1

CW

Printed in the United States of America

Contents

Summer Olympic Events   vii
Summer Olympic Games   x

Introduction
Let the Games Begin!   1

Chapter One
Marathon   4

Chapter Two
Men's Short-Distance Races   12

Chapter Three
Women's Short-Distance Races   21

Chapter Four
Men's and Women's Field Events   28

Chapter Five
Men's and Women's Long-Distance Races   36

Chapter Six
Decathlon and Heptathlon   42

Chapter Seven
Women's Gymnastics   50

Chapter Eight
Men's Gymnastics   63

Chapter Nine
Women's Swimming   77

Chapter Ten
Men's Swimming   88

Chapter Eleven
The Greatest Olympic Athlete in History (So Far!)   98

★ SUMMER OLYMPIC EVENTS ★

Aquatics (synchronized swimming for women only)

Archery

Athletics/Track and Field (decathlon for men only; heptathlon for women only)

Badminton

Basketball

Boxing (women's boxing included for 2012)

Canoeing

Cycling

Equestrian

Fencing

Football/Soccer

Golf

Gymnastics

Handball

Hockey

Judo

Modern pentathlon

Rowing

Rugby

Sailing

Shooting

Table tennis

Tae kwon do

Tennis

Triathlon

Volleyball

Weight lifting

Wrestling

★ EVENTS[1] INCLUDED IN EVERY ★
OLYMPICS FROM 1896[2] TO PRESENT

100-meter dash

110-meter hurdles

---

[1] Only men took part in the first Olympics; women were not included.

[2] Also on the program since 1896 were two rowing events, single sculls and eight-oared shell with coxswain, but they were canceled in 1896 because of foul weather.

400-meter dash

800-meter run

1,500-meter run

Discus throw

High jump

Long jump

Marathon

Pole vault

Shot put

Triple jump

Individual foil fencing

Individual sabre fencing

1,200-meter freestyle swimming

✯ SUMMER OLYMPIC GAMES ✯

NOC: National Olympic Committee (Each country with Olympic teams officially recognized by the International Olympic Committee, or IOC, has a National Olympic Committee.)

April 6–15, 1896: Athens, Greece
14 NOCs, 241 athletes (all men), 43 events

May 14–October 28, 1900: Paris, France
24 NOCs, 997 athletes, 95 events

July 1–November 23, 1904: St. Louis, Missouri, United States
12 NOCs, 651 athletes, 91 events

April 27–October 31, 1908: London, England
22 NOCs, 2,008 athletes, 110 events

May 5–July 27, 1912: Stockholm, Sweden
28 NOCs, 2,407 athletes, 102 events

1916: Berlin, Germany (canceled because of World War I)

April 20–September 12, 1920: Antwerp, Belgium
29 NOCs (Germany and four other countries were not invited to participate), 2,626 athletes, 154 events

May 4–July 27, 1924: Paris, France
44 NOCs (Germany was not invited), 3,089 athletes, 126 events

May 17–August 12, 1928: Amsterdam, the Netherlands
46 NOCs, 2,883 athletes, 109 events

July 30–August 14, 1932: Los Angeles, California, United States
37 NOCs, 1,332 athletes, 117 events

August 1–16, 1936: Berlin, Germany
49 NOCs, 3,963 athletes, 129 events

1940: Tokyo, Japan, then Helsinki, Finland (canceled because of World War II)

1944: London, England (canceled because of World War II)

July 29–August 14, 1948: London, England
59 NOCs (Germany, and Japan, who had lost World War II, were not invited; the Soviet Union did not attend), 4,104 athletes, 136 events

July 19–August 3, 1952: Helsinki, Finland
69 NOCs, 4,955 athletes, 149 events

November 22–December 8, 1956: Melbourne, Australia (Equestrian held in Stockholm, Sweden)
72 NOCs, 3,314 athletes, 145 events

August 25–September 11, 1960: Rome, Italy
83 NOCs, 5,338 athletes, 150 events

October 10–24, 1964: Tokyo, Japan
93 NOCs (South Africa is banned because of apartheid and not allowed back until 1992; Indonesia and North Korea pull out over issues with the IOC), 5,151 athletes, 163 events

October 12–27, 1968: Mexico City, Mexico
112 NOCs, 5,516 athletes, 172 events

August 26–September 11, 1972: Munich, West Germany
121 NOCs, 7,134 athletes, 195 events

July 17–August 1, 1976: Montreal, Canada
92 NOCs (Twenty-two African NOCs boycotted in protest of the New Zealand rugby team's tour of apartheid South Africa), 6,084 athletes, 198 events

July 19–August 3, 1980: Moscow, Soviet Union
80 NOCs (Lowest number of NOCs since 1956; the United States and 64 other countries, including athletic

powerhouses West Germany and Japan, boycotted in response to the Soviet Union's invasion of Afghanistan), 5,179 athletes, 203 events

July 28–August 12, 1984: Los Angeles, California, United States
140 NOCs (The Soviet Union boycotted in retaliation for the 1980 U.S. boycott), 6,829 athletes, 221 events

September 17–October 2, 1988: Seoul, South Korea
159 NOCs (North Korea boycotted, as did Cuba, Ethiopia, and Nicaragua, after host country South Korea becomes a democracy to get to host the Olympics), 8,391 athletes, 237 events

July 25–August 9, 1992: Barcelona, Spain
169 NOCs (no boycotts; South Africa was invited after apartheid was abolished; the Berlin Wall had fallen, uniting Germany; and the Soviet Union had disbanded into twenty-five countries), 9,356 athletes, 257 events

July 19–August 4, 1996: Atlanta, Georgia, United States
197 NOCs, 10,318 athletes, 271 events

September 15–October 1, 2000: Sydney, Australia
199 NOCs, 10,651 athletes, 300 events

August 13–29, 2004: Athens, Greece
201 NOCs, 10,625 athletes, 301 events

August 8–24, 2008: Beijing, China
204 NOCs, 10,942 athletes, 302 events

July 27–August 12, 2012: London, England
Information not yet available

August 5–21, 2016: Rio de Janeiro, Brazil
Information not yet available

GREAT MOMENTS IN THE
SUMMER OLYMPICS

✷ INTRODUCTION ✷

Let the Games Begin!

The world's greatest international sports competition, the Olympic Games, began more than a century ago on November 25, 1892. That's when a French baron named Pierre de Coubertin presented his idea to resurrect the ancient Greek sporting tradition of the same name to a group of his colleagues. Four years and a great deal of work later, his idea came to life with the first Games of the modern era. Two hundred forty-one athletes—all men—from fourteen nations traveled to Athens, Greece, to compete in forty-three events. First-place winners were awarded laurel wreaths, diplomas, and silver medals.

From 1896, the Olympics grew steadily into one of the largest and most anticipated international competitions in the world. In 1924, they were separated into Summer and Winter Games with both competitions held in the same calendar year. That format stuck until 1992, when the Games were alternated every two years—the next Winter Games took place in 1994 and the next Summer Games in 1996.

No matter their sport or season, Olympic hopefuls train long and hard for the opportunity to represent their countries in the Games. Those who qualify are the best of the best from their nation. Win or lose, they all have earned a place in Olympic history.

There are those, however, whose stories rise above all others. These are the men and women who astonished the public with their athletic triumphs—or captured its sympathy with their heart-wrenching failures. No book can hope to retell all these moments, for there have simply been too many. The Summer Games alone have hundreds of highlights.

There's the story of the 1948 gold medalist sharpshooter Karoly Takacs who later learned to fire a gun with his left hand after suffering a crippling injury to his right—and then won his second gold medal in 1952 with left-handed shooting. In 1988, diver Greg Louganis struck his head on the springboard and yet came back to win gold in that event and the platform, the first male to post an Olympic "double-double" in diving. Laszlo Papp, Felix Savon, and Teofilo Stevenson share a place in the record books as the only boxers to win three golds in three straight Games.

Wrestlers, equestrians, basketball players, soccer players, cyclists—the list of amazing Olympians goes on and on. So rather than try to mention them all, this book focuses on the three most popular and storied disciplines from the Summer Games: athletics, also known as track and field; gymnastics; and swimming. Each chapter retells special moments that captivated the world and catapulted the athletes to fame.

So turn the page and, as the old saying goes: Let the Games begin!

✮ CHAPTER ONE ✮

Marathon

In the early fall of 490 BC, Persia invaded the Greek town of Marathon. A Persian victory seemed certain, for the Persian soldiers outnumbered the Greeks almost three to one. The invaders would then have a clear shot at Athens, the heart of the Greek civilization. If Athens fell, Greece itself would likely fall.

Against all odds, the Greeks won the Battle of Marathon. A messenger called Pheidippides (also known as Philippides) was ordered to Athens to proclaim the victory. Legend has it that he ran the entire way, a distance of more than forty kilometers. When he reached the city, he announced the good news, and then collapsed and died. From that event, we get the word *marathon*, a race of forty kilometers, or about twenty-five miles. (The distance of the marathon was changed to 26.2 miles in 1908 for the Olympic Games in London, England.)

This long-distance race would later become the highlight of the 1896 Games in Athens, Greece. On April 10, seventeen runners took off toward Athens from Marathon, retracing Pheidippides's route. Few had ever run so far. Their inexperience soon showed. One by one, they dropped out, too exhausted to continue. Finally, only a handful remained.

Throughout the race, messengers updated spectators in the stadium of the racers' progress. Soon after the thirty-kilometer mark, they announced that an Australian had the lead. A wave of disappointment rippled through the stands. The Greeks had hoped that one of their countrymen might win the historic event.

Then a man on horseback galloped into the stadium. He rode straight for the royal box, where he informed Greece's King George and his family that a Greek was now the front-runner!

Excitement surged throughout the stadium when a twenty-four-year-old Greek shepherd named Spiridon Louis entered the arena; not even the royals were able to contain their joy. Crown Prince Constantine and his brother George flanked Louis to the finish line. Two hours, fifty-eight minutes, and fifty seconds after his start, Louis crossed that line—and into the history books as the first winner of the Olympic marathon.

The 1896 marathon had proved that not *every* runner was up to the challenge of such a long-distance race. An Italian athlete hammered home that fact at the 1908 London Games.

Dorando Pietri was the first runner to enter the stadium that year. The finish line was a mere 385 yards away. But instead of dashing across to victory, Pietri staggered in the wrong direction. Then he collapsed. For a long minute, no one knew what to do. If track officials helped him, he'd be disqualified. So they decided to see whether he could finish under his own power.

Somehow, Pietri got back on his feet, only to collapse again. This agonizing scene played out four more times before officials intervened and half carried the exhausted runner over the finish line. Their aid helped Pietri finish the race (and may have saved his life), but it cost him the gold medal.

Long-distance runners typically train for many months to prepare for the grueling challenge of a marathon. But every so often, there comes an athlete who just seems born to run. At the 1952 Games in Helsinki, Finland, that athlete was Emil Zatopek from Czechoslovakia.

Zatopek had an unusual running style that made him look as if he were in extreme pain. "I was not talented enough to run and smile at the same time," he once joked. At the 1948 London Games, that running style earned him an Olympic record in the 10,000-meter race with a time of twenty-nine minutes and 59.6 seconds (29:59.6). He also took home a silver medal in the 5,000-meter race.

Four years later, he broke his own record in the 10,000-meter by improving his time to 29:17.0 and then also broke the 5,000-meter record. With two gold medals to his credit already, he made an unbelievable last-minute decision to enter the marathon — despite never having run one before!

Zatopek later joked that he had entered the race because his wife, Dana Ingrova Zatopkova, had just won a gold medal in the javelin throw — making them the first husband-wife Olympic gold medalists — and he wanted to outdo her three golds to one. Whether that was true or not, he accomplished his goal. He breezed through the marathon with effortless

7

grace. While other runners withdrew from exhaustion, he chatted with bike messengers and spectators along the route. He not only won the race but also set his third Olympic record of 1952 with a time of two hours, twenty-three minutes, and 3.2 seconds (2:23:03.2). He was the first person to take gold in the 5,000-meter, 10,000-meter, and marathon races in a single Olympic Games.

Eight years after Zatopek's historic marathon, all eyes were on an Ethiopian runner who approached the race in a new way—barefoot! Abebe Bikila was not favored to win the 1960 event in Rome, Italy, but he had a secret plan.

Not far from the finish line, the race route took runners past the ancient obelisk of Axum, a tall granite pillar that had been stolen from Ethiopia during World War II. Bikila thought the plundered landmark would be a fitting place for a burst of speed. So when he reached the obelisk, he stepped up his pace and took the lead. He won the marathon with a world best time of 2:15:16.2 and also entered the history books as the first black African to win a gold medal.

Amazingly, Bikila—now wearing running shoes—beat his own record at the 1964 Games in Tokyo, Japan. His time was 2:12:11.2, earning him a place in Olympic history as the first person to win back-to-back marathons. As a reward for his efforts, his government gave him a car. Five years later, he was behind the wheel of that same car when tragedy struck. He crashed, breaking his neck and severing his spinal cord. Fortunately he survived the accident, but he was paralyzed from the waist down for the remainder of his life.

The field of marathon runners has grown significantly since Spiridon Louis's time. By 1992, 112 athletes from seventy-two nations lined up at the start in Barcelona, Spain. Among them were Hwang Young-Cho from South Korea and Koichi Morishita from Japan. Throughout the last section of the race, the two ran neck-and-neck. Then, at the final two-kilometer mark, Young-Cho sped up just enough to take the lead for good. He crossed the finish line with a time of 2:13:23 and then buckled to his knees. He was too tired to take the traditional victory lap, but his wide smile let everyone know how happy he was.

Among those watching was fellow marathon winner and countryman Sohn Kee-Chung. Kee-Chung won the demanding race in 1936. At that time, Korea was occupied by Japan, so Kee-Chung was forced to compete under the Japanese flag. Now, more than five decades later, he beamed with pride as the South Korean flag flew in Young-Cho's honor.

To date, no Olympian has broken the two-hour mark, although at the 2008 Games in Beijing, China, Samuel Wanjiru of Kenya came close with a time of 2:06:32. That was a new Olympic record, better by nearly three minutes than the previous time set by Carlos Lopes at the 1984 Games in Los Angeles, California.

Lopes was not the only marathon winner at the Games that year. For the first time, women competed in a marathon of their own. Before 1984, the International Olympic Committee (IOC) considered women too fragile for the grueling race—even though female runners had covered the distance many times before. In fact, some believe that in 1896, two Greek women ran the course.

Nearly a century later, the inaugural women's marathon was held. It wasn't much of a competition, however. The winner, American Joan Benoit, established an early lead and then cruised to victory virtually unchallenged. Her time of 2:24:52 held until 2000, when the current Olympic-record holder, Japan's Naoko Takahashi, finished the race in 2:23:14.

Spiridon Louis once said that winning the marathon was "something unimaginable...like a dream." Regardless of whether women or men run that race, one thing is certain: The longest distance event in the Olympics has provided decades of inspiring stories of athletes who pushed themselves to their greatest limit.

⋆ CHAPTER TWO ⋆

Men's Short-Distance Races

What would it be like to be the fastest runner in the world? In 1936, American Jesse Owens found out.

The 1936 Olympics were held in Berlin, Germany, under the watchful eye of Adolf Hitler. In the years before these Games, Hitler had used a potent combination of military might, brutality, and intense propaganda to gain power and promote his Nazi agenda. A big piece of Hitler's agenda was to define which kinds of people were "good" and which were "bad." According to Hitler, good people were of the Aryan race—that is, blond, blue-eyed Christians. The list of "bad" people included Jews, blacks, and homosexuals—basically anyone Hitler felt threatened his vision of a powerful, racially pure German state.

Hitler realized the Games could be the perfect showcase for his Aryan agenda. He believed that his athletes would emerge victorious over all other competitors and would prove the superiority of their race.

Things did not go according to Hitler's plan, however. Jesse Owens, a twenty-two-year-old African American, completely debunked Hitler's claim that blacks were physically inferior by turning in the best track and field performance of any athlete at the time.

Owens had just missed making the U.S. Olympic team in 1932, but in 1936 he emerged as its star. He blew away the other runners in the 100-meter dash with a time of 10.3 seconds. He captured another gold medal and set an Olympic record in the 200-meter final two days later, crossing the finish line in 20.7 seconds. In between, he leaped to an Olympic record in the long jump, a distance of 8.06 meters (26.4 feet). His long jump success was even more remarkable because he nearly didn't qualify for the event!

Owens, like all the long jumpers, had three attempts to qualify. He fouled on the first two when his foot touched the takeoff line. One more mistake and he would have been eliminated.

Help came from an unexpected source, a German long jumper named Luz Long. Long was the very image of Aryanism — blond, blue-eyed, and in peak physical condition. He was the perfect example for Hitler's agenda, but he didn't believe in Hitler's values. When he saw Owens having trouble, he offered to put his towel on the ground a foot in front of the line. Long suggested that if Owens jumped from there, he wouldn't foul. Owens took Long up on his offer, qualified with ease, and later jumped to gold. A true sportsman, Long was the first person to congratulate Owens.

"We walked arm-in-arm right in front of Hitler's box. Hitler must have gone crazy watching us embrace," Owens once said.

In the second week of the Games, Owens earned his fourth gold medal as a controversial substitute on the 4×100-meter relay team. The original foursome included two Jewish runners, Marty Glickman and Sam Stoller. Shortly before the final, the U.S. coaches abruptly replaced Glickman and Stoller with Owens and teammate Ralph Metcalfe. While no one knows for sure why they made the switches, most believe they bowed to pressure from the Nazi organizers. Owens's protests on his teammates' behalf fell on deaf ears. He ran the first leg of the race, giving his team such a large lead that they won by more than thirteen meters.

Before Jesse Owens's great triumphs, there had been other amazing sprinters, too. In 1900, American Alvin Kraenzlein tore up sixty meters of track in 7 seconds. His world record stands today because the 60-meter event was cut from the Olympics after the 1904 Games.

Two decades later, at the 1924 Games in Paris, France, Harold Abrahams of Great Britain perfected his stride by laying pieces of paper on the ground where he wanted his feet to fall. He knew he had hit the marks when his spikes picked up the papers. His training paid off, for in the 100-meter dash he equaled the Olympic record of 10.6 seconds to win gold.

That same year, Abrahams's teammate Eric Liddell astonished the crowd by running the second half of the 400-meter race at such a fast pace that his competitors were literally stumbling to keep up.

"I don't like to be beaten," Liddell once said of his performance. His and Abrahams's Olympic stories were later turned into an Oscar-winning movie, *Chariots of Fire*, and although the film didn't get all the facts right, it did inspire many future runners.

Another pair of sprinters provided a different kind of inspiration at the 1968 Olympics in Mexico City, Mexico. In the 200-meter race, American Tommie Smith broke the tape with a world-record time of 19.83 seconds. His teammate John Carlos crossed .27 seconds later, good enough for the bronze. Their races were impressive, but it was what they did during the medal ceremony that left a lasting impression.

Smith and Carlos, both African Americans, were members of a group called the Olympic Project for Human Rights. The project's goal was to expose the discrimination against African Americans in the United States. As "The Star-Spangled Banner" began to play, they raised clenched fists and bowed their heads. The gesture was the Black Power salute, a symbol of silent protest and solidarity for their fellow African Americans.

By today's standards, the salute seems tame. But back then it sent out shockwaves of fury. Smith and Carlos were pulled from their remaining events and ordered to leave the Olympic Village. They faced harsh criticism in the media. But they stood by their unspoken statement—and in time, the world took a different, more understanding view of their actions.

At the 1984 Games in Los Angeles, an electrifying

new Olympic track and field star sprinted onto the scene. Carl Lewis of the U.S. team started his reign of the Athletics competition with a gold medal in the 100-meter race. He added a second gold medal with a long jump of 8.54 meters (28 feet). A third gold was hung around his neck following the 200-meter race.

His final event was the 4×100-meter relay. If his team took gold there, Lewis would duplicate Jesse Owens's feat of 1936.

The 4×100-meter relay demands teamwork and timing as well as speed. The first runner carries a baton and sprints to meet the second runner. He has to pass the baton within a certain stretch of track. If he doesn't pass it in time, the team is disqualified. If either runner drops the baton, they lose precious seconds off their team total and risk disqualification if the baton falls outside the lane. The second runner continues with the baton and passes it to the third, who races with it to the fourth, or anchor. The anchor sprints the last leg with one purpose in mind: to break the tape.

In 1936, Jesse Owens ran first. He was so fast he gave his team an insurmountable lead. In 1984, Carl Lewis, however, ran anchor. When teammate Calvin Smith slapped the baton into his hand, Lewis took off like a bullet. He covered the final distance in 8.94 seconds. The team's total time was a world record of 37.83 seconds. Lewis had replicated Owens's four track and field gold medals in one Olympics!

That was the end of Lewis's medals — for that year's competition, anyway. He returned to the Games again in 1988. There he added two more golds: one for the 100-meter dash, the other in the long jump. He actually crossed the finish line second in the race but was awarded gold when the first-place runner, Canadian Ben Johnson, later tested positive for performance-enhancing drugs. Lewis might have won a third medal for the 4×100-meter relay, but his team was disqualified for passing the baton out of the zone. He earned a silver in the 200-meter dash that year to bring his two-Olympics total to six golds and one silver.

And he wasn't finished yet. In 1992 and 1996, he out-jumped the competition to become the third individual to win the same event four times in a row. When he raced to victory as part of the 4×100-meter relay squad, he earned another place in the Olympic history books as the fourth person to earn nine gold medals.

The 1992 Barcelona Games were supposed to

feature another outstanding American sprinter. From the spring of 1990 to the early summer of 1992, Michael Johnson had won thirty-two straight 200-meter races. He was even more dominant in the 400-meter, capturing firsts in fifty-four straight races from 1989 to 1996. He was scheduled to run both events in 1992, but a bad case of food poisoning left him so weak he had to withdraw. He recovered enough to help the 4×400-relay team bring home gold, however.

After his disappointment in the 1992 Games, Johnson exploded on the scene at the 1996 Olympics in Atlanta, Georgia. Wearing an eye-catching pair of gold running shoes, he blew away the competition in the 400-meter dash to set an Olympic record of 43.49 seconds. He was so fast that when he broke the tape, the second-place runner was still ten meters behind him!

At the start of the 200-meter race, Johnson faltered a bit but then took control. Unbelievably, he increased his speed with each passing meter. When he crossed the finish line, he became the first athlete to win the 200-meter and the 400-meter races in a single Olympics. He had also set a new world record of 19.32 seconds, a full .34 less than his own world record!

"When I saw 19.32 seconds on the clock, I couldn't believe it," he told reporters.

Others were equally amazed. "That's not a time," the third-place runner, Ato Boldon, marveled. "It sounds like my dad's birthday."

Johnson defended his 400-meter title at the 2000 Olympics in Sydney, Australia, the only male in Olympic history to win that event twice in a row.

In 2008, Jamaican sprinter Usain "Lightning" Bolt flashed onto the Olympic scene. Bolt set Olympic and world records for the 100-meter dash, 200-meter dash, and 4×100-meter relay. Footage of his individual races shows him running so far in front of his challengers that it looks as if he had a head start.

☆ CHAPTER THREE ☆

Women's Short-Distance Races

After the first men's-only Olympics in 1896, women slowly but steadily gained a foothold in the Games. By 1924, they'd competed in tennis, golf, archery, fencing, swimming, and equestrian events, among others. But despite petitions to include them, no track and field events were held for women.

That changed in 1928, when the IOC reluctantly agreed to add two races, the 100-meter dash and the 800-meter run, to the women's program. The second of those two races proved nearly disastrous, for after the final, many of the runners collapsed from exhaustion. The IOC took that as proof that such an event was too much for women to handle. They banned the 800-meter run and any future races longer than two hundred meters from the Games; it wasn't until 1960 that longer distances were reintroduced.

The 100-meter race was the first female track event. The winner, a sixteen-year-old American named Elizabeth "Betty" Robinson, emerged as the top female Olympic sprinter. Amazingly, she was only in the Olympics thanks to sheer luck.

Robinson was a high school student in Illinois when a teacher spotted her running to catch a train. The teacher was so impressed that he asked if he could time her running down a school hallway. She agreed—and was as stunned as he was at how fast she covered the distance. She began training with the high school boys' track team. Less than a year later, she qualified for the Olympics. At the 1928 Games in Amsterdam, the Netherlands, she not only won the gold medal, but she also set the world record with a time of 12.2 seconds. She took silver as part of the 4×100-relay team that year, too.

Robinson was looking forward to a second Olympic outing in 1932. But the year before those Games, she was in a terrible plane crash that left her with severe injuries including a broken leg and a shattered hip. The man who found her believed she was dead. He placed her in the trunk of his car and brought her to a nearby mortician. Thankfully, the mortician quickly discovered she was still alive!

Remarkably, Robinson recovered from her injuries enough to race in the 1936 Berlin Olympics. Although she couldn't bend her leg to get into the starter's crouch for the 100-meter race, she was part of the gold medal–winning 4×100-meter relay team.

That Olympics marked the first appearance of a future running star. Those who saw Fanny Koen of the Netherlands then might never have suspected what she would one day achieve — her performance was not very impressive. She herself once said the highlight for her that year was getting Jesse Owens's autograph.

Undeterred by her poor results, Koen set her sights on the next Olympics. But the 1940 and 1944 Games were canceled because of World War II. When the Olympics finally resumed in 1948, twelve years had passed. In that time, Koen had turned thirty, married her coach Jan Blankers, and started a family. The idea that she would compete in the 1948 London Games seemed laughable to many.

But not to Blankers-Koen. She believed in herself and trained to win. Win is exactly what she did, too, and in a big, big way. She entered four events — the 100-meter race, the 80-meter hurdles (expanded to 100 meters in 1972), the 200-meter race, and the

4×100-meter relay—and took gold in each! She remains today the only woman to collect four firsts in track and field in a single Olympics.

Twelve years after Blankers-Koen astonished the sporting world, another female runner took center stage. When Wilma Rudolph was born in 1940, she was so tiny that no one was sure whether she would live. When she was later left partially paralyzed by bouts of pneumonia, scarlet fever, and polio, no one knew if she would walk right again.

But Rudolph's family didn't give up on her. Instead, they took turns massaging her crippled leg until she could walk with a brace and, later, with a corrective shoe. By the time she was eleven, she had tossed the shoe aside. And at age sixteen she wasn't just walking— she was running fast enough to earn a place on the U.S. Olympic team.

"If it wasn't for my family," Rudolph later said, "I probably would never have been able to walk properly, no less run."

Rudolph earned a bronze medal at the 1956 Games in Melbourne, Australia, as part of the 4×100-meter relay. In 1960, she qualified for the 100-meter dash, the 200-meter dash, and the 4×100-meter relay. Dubbed the Black Gazelle, the Black Pearl, and the

World's Fastest Woman by the press, Rudolph won each event—the first American woman to come home with three gold medals in a single Olympics.

Rudolph never participated in another Olympics, but she inspired many other female runners to try for gold. One of them was Wyomia Tyus, who in 1964 and 1968 became the first woman to win back-to-back 100-meter dashes. Another was the great Florence Griffith Joyner, better known as Flo Jo.

Flo Jo first hit the Olympic track in 1984. She was a strong runner, good enough to take silver in the 200-meter race, although that year her long fingernails drew more comments than her stride. The next Olympics, however, few people paid attention to her hands because they were too busy trying to watch her feet.

Flo Jo had spent the four years since the 1984 Los Angeles Games studying films of Carl Lewis and other top male sprinters and then putting what she'd learned into practice. In the 1988 Games in Seoul, South Korea, her training paid off. She broke the tape in the 100-meter dash with a gold medal–winning time of 10.54 seconds. Later, she raced to a second gold and a world record in the 200-meter race with a time of 21.32 seconds, a full .7 seconds better than her previous Olympic time. When she won a third gold medal as part of the 4×100-meter relay, her name was added to the short list of elite female runners. Sadly, Flo Jo died in her sleep ten years after her Olympic triumphs. She was just thirty-eight years old.

In 1992, yet another American woman dashed her way to the top ranks of female Olympic sprinters. Gail Devers (her full name was Yolanda Gail Devers) was training for the 1988 Games when she began to suffer from a wide range of physical ailments. Headaches, weight loss, blurred vision, muscle pulls—as the list grew, Devers had to drop out.

For the next two years, Devers searched for a diagnosis for her condition. She finally got one. She had Graves' disease, a malfunction of the thyroid gland. Radiation treatments controlled the condition but left her with bleeding, cracked, and swollen feet. She could barely walk, let alone run.

Yet Devers refused to give up her Olympic dream. "The word *quit* has never been part of my vocabulary," she once said. So as her feet slowly recovered, she began to train again. When the 1992 Games opened in Barcelona, she was there.

Devers ran in two events that year, the 100-meter race and the 100-meter hurdles. She placed fifth in the hurdles, but she made headlines in the dash. The finish of that race was so close that the judges had to rely on the instant replay to decide a winner. After much deliberation, they declared that Devers had beaten the second-place runner by a mere .01 seconds!

★ CHAPTER FOUR ★

Men's and Women's Field Events

On April 6, 1896, American James Connolly jumped into sports history as the first athlete since AD 369 to win an Olympic event. That event was the triple jump, then known as two hops and a jump (or sometimes a hop, skip, and jump). Connolly annihilated the competition, clearing a total distance of 13.71 meters (45 feet). By comparison, the second-place jump fell short of Connolly's mark by a full meter, or more than three feet!

When it came to jumping, American Ray Ewry outdid all others in three straight Olympics. He is near the top of the list of all-time Olympic gold medal winners — and yet few people have heard of him. That's because the events he competed in, the standing high jump, the standing long jump, and the standing triple jump, were discontinued after the 1904 Games (standing triple jump) and 1912 Games (standing high jump and standing long jump). As the names indicate, these jumps were made without a run up. The athlete was allowed just one step before leaving the ground.

That few people have ever heard of Ewry is a shame because his story is the stuff of legends. He was orphaned at the age of five. Two years later, he contracted polio. The disease left him without the use of his legs and confined to a wheelchair. Most doctors told him he'd never walk again. But one suggested that if he exercised his leg muscles, he might get out of his wheelchair someday.

Ewry took that suggestion to heart, and slowly but surely, his legs grew stronger. They became so strong that he not only walked again, but also became the world's greatest standing jumper. Ewry won gold medals in the three standing jump events in both 1900 and 1904. The standing triple jump was off the program after 1904, but in 1908, he added two more golds in the remaining standing jump events.

Eight gold medals! And counting the gold from his championship jumps at the Intercalated Games in Athens in 1906—an intermediary Olympics that the IOC doesn't officially recognize but that was in all other ways a true Olympics — his final gold medal total is an unbelievable ten!

To understand just how remarkable Ewry's jumping ability was, consider this: In his 1900 gold medal high jump, he jumped straight up, knees bent to his chest, so that his feet cleared a height of 1.655 meters (5.4 feet). That's the height of a typical adult woman!

American discus thrower Alfred Oerter may not have earned as many gold medals as Ray Ewry, but he did achieve Olympic greatness in his discipline. Oerter had started out as a sprinter, but when he was fifteen, he threw a discus for the first time. His throw was so good that his track coach suggested he switch. Oerter did, and five years later, he earned his first gold medal at the 1956 Melbourne Olympics with a record-breaking throw of 56.36 meters (184.9 feet).

Oerter's career — and his life — nearly ended in a car crash the next year. But true champion that he was, he didn't give up on himself. By 1960, he was ready to compete again.

And compete he did! Oerter returned to the next three Olympics and claimed gold in each. Unlike some athletes, who burn bright early only to flame out later, Oerter just got better. In 1964, he entered the history books as the first discus thrower to hit 61 meters (200.1 feet). He bested his own records at each Olympics, ending his run in 1968 with a distance of 64.78 meters (212.5 feet).

Oerter didn't compete in another Olympics after 1968. But there's little doubt that if he had, he could have added to his winning streak, for he continued to train and improve. Some of his longest throws came after he turned forty. One throw, done for a television documentary, would have been a world record had it been official. Ever the competitor, he joked in 1996 that he might set his sights on the 2000 Games in Sydney, warning, "Don't count me out!"

While Oerter was throwing his way into the record books in 1968, another American was taking a page from Olympic history to help him win a gold medal. Long jumper Robert Beamon had won twenty-two out of twenty-three competitions that year. But like Jesse Owens years earlier, he was on the brink of fouling out of the event. Luckily, he was reminded of Owens's solution—setting down a takeoff marker before the actual takeoff board—and decided to try the same thing. It worked; Beamon made it to the final round. And yet, he was still plagued by such doubts that as he began his approach, he told himself "don't foul, don't foul," over and over.

He didn't foul. Instead, he jumped farther than any Olympian ever had, a distance of 8.9 meters (29.2 feet)! He was so shocked by his accomplishment that his body shut down and he dropped to his knees, a phenomenon known as cataplectic seizure. It turned out he had every right to be overwhelmed — as of the 2008 Olympics, no one has beaten his record.

Beamon wasn't the only American athlete with a surprise up his sleeve. In another field event, one of his teammates was turning heads with a new style of jumping.

In 1962, Dick Fosbury was a fifteen-year-old mediocre track athlete who had trouble clearing the high jump bar. He tried several of the accepted jumping styles, including the straddle and the western roll, but nothing worked. Then one practice, desperate to get over, he unconsciously changed his posture. Instead of diving over facedown, he began twisting so he faced up, arching his back midway into his jump to help pull his lower half up and over. In that one afternoon, he improved his clearance by an astonishing six inches!

Six years later, he introduced the "Fosbury flop" to the world at the Mexico City Olympics. His unique style might have been laughed off had he not won the gold with it. Other athletes copied his technique, and by 1980, practically every high jumper was doing the flop.

If the Fosbury flop had been invented decades earlier, it might have saved a female track star from having to accept silver instead of gold for her jump. Mildred "Babe" Didrikson was a gifted athlete who might have easily won five gold medals in 1932 if she had been allowed to enter all the events that she'd qualified for. But back then, the IOC believed women weren't strong enough to compete in more than three events. So Didrikson was forced to limit herself to the javelin, the 80-meter hurdles, and the high jump.

First up was the javelin. It was the first time this event was open to women. Didrikson did her gender proud, hurling for a distance of 43.68 meters (143.3 feet). That was good enough for gold, though shy of the world record. "I could have thrown it a lot farther if it hadn't slipped in my hand," she told reporters later.

Next, Didrikson ran the hurdles. She was fast, but her teammate Evelyne Hall was just as swift. The two crossed the finish line at almost exactly the same moment. After much deliberation, however, the judges awarded the gold medal to Didrikson. Hall protested, pointing to a mark on her neck she said had been made when she broke the tape. But the judges stood by their decision.

Didrikson's third event was the high jump. There, she and Jean Shiley cleared the exact same distance of 1.657 meters (5.4 feet). Again, the judges had to intervene to determine which woman had won. They returned a decision that delighted Shiley as much as it outraged Didrikson. They claimed that because Didrikson's head cleared the bar before her body, her last jump was illegal.

"That's the way I jumped during the whole competition," Didrikson pointed out. "If I was illegal on my last jump, I was illegal on my first jump. So if they were right, I should have been disqualified from the beginning." But as with Hall's, Didrikson's protests fell on deaf ears. She had to be content with silver rather than gold.

Almost half a century later, the 1980 women's long jump competition saw one of the greatest come-from-behind victories in the history of the sport. When Tatiana Skachko of the Soviet Union jumped 7.01 meters (23 feet), she seemed the hands-down winner. But then the impossible happened. Tatiana

Kolpakova, an unknown Soviet athlete, leaped 7.06 meters (23.2 feet). Skachko dropped to second place — and then to third when Brigitte Wujak of East Germany jumped 7.04 meters (23.1 feet).

Of her triumph, Kolpakova summed it up by stating the obvious: "One should always fight until the end."

That's just what Jackie Joyner-Kersee — sister-in-law of Florence "Flo Jo" Joyner — did in Seoul eight years later. In the opening round of the long jump final, Joyner-Kersee was in second when she fouled on her fourth attempt. That's when her coach and husband, Bob Kersee, gave her a boost of confidence by saying he thought she "had 7.4" in her. On her fifth and final jump, she hit exactly that number. That 24.3-foot leap set a new Olympic record!

⭐ CHAPTER FIVE ⭐

Men's and Women's Long-Distance Races

The 1952 Helsinki Olympics saw the return of one of the greatest endurance runners of all time. Paavo Nurmi, otherwise known as the Flying Finn, was fifty-five years old when he entered the stadium — not as a competitor, but as a link in the Olympic torch run. Spectators rose to their feet in a standing ovation, honoring the glory of his past accomplishments.

And they were indeed glorious. At the 1920 Games in Antwerp, Belgium, he won three long-distance events: the 10,000-meter run, the 8,000-meter individual cross-country run, and the cross-country team run; he also took silver for the 5,000-meter run. Four years later, he astonished the sporting world again with what he did in a single day.

In Paris, on July 10, 1924, Nurmi blew away the competition in the 1,500-meter run. Then, less than an hour later—hardly enough time for his body to recover—he lined up for the start of the 5,000-meter run.

Also in the lineup was fellow Finn Ville Ritola. Ritola had replaced Nurmi as the 10,000-meter champ that year after officials prevented Nurmi from entering, fearing his health would suffer if he took part in too many long-distance events. Nurmi wanted nothing more than to surpass Ritola now.

The race was thrilling from start to finish. When the starting gun went off, Ritola sprinted into the lead. "Paavo tried to pass me, but I held him off," Ritola remembered later. "For any other runner... that would have been the end of it."

But Nurmi wasn't "any other runner," a fact made evident by his unorthodox habit of carrying a stopwatch to time his pace during races. Midway through the final lap, he checked that watch and then tossed it aside, picked up speed, and surged ahead of Ritola to win by two-tenths of a second. "I could not believe that after running the 1,500 earlier, he still had the strength," Ritola marveled. "But he did."

Nurmi went on to win three more gold medals in Paris to bring his two-Olympics total to eight golds and one silver. Two of his 1924 victories were for the

8,000-meter individual cross-country and the cross-country team race, events that proved so punishing to the athletes that they were dropped from the program after that year. He added yet another gold—in the 10,000-meter run, beating out Ritola—plus two more silvers in 1928 in Amsterdam, the Netherlands. With twelve total, Nurmi earned a place in the list of top-five male gold medal winners of modern Olympic history, a spot he still retains as of 2008.

While Nurmi amazed with his ability, another runner inspired with his will to win. No one expected American Billy Mills to finish in the top three, let alone win, the 10,000-meter run in 1964. After all, his competition included record-holder Ron Clarke from Australia and Mohamed Gammoudi from Tunisia. Sure enough, as the race reached the final lap, Clarke was in the lead with Gammoudi not far behind.

Mills wasn't out of it yet. But his chances for breaking the tape looked slim, for the lanes in front of him were clogged with runners whom he had lapped. But Clarke and Gammoudi were blocked by those slower runners, too. Desperate to get ahead, Clarke nudged Mills aside to try to open a path. Mills stumbled, but Clarke didn't get the advantage because at that same

moment Gammoudi pushed himself between them —
and into first place!

Clarke caught up to Gammoudi after a few steps,
and together they sprinted toward the finish line.
The roars of seventy-five thousand fans filled their
ears as they drew closer. But it turned out those roars
weren't for them, but for Billy Mills!

"Look at Mills! Look at Mills!" one announcer
screamed incredulously. With arms and legs churn-
ing, Mills came from behind and motored past Clarke
and Gammoudi to victory!

Years later, Mills laughingly recalled the moments
after his win. "The Japanese official came up to me . . .
and he's asking me over and over again as he's shak-
ing me, 'Who are you? Who are you?' And my thoughts
were, 'Oh my God, did I miscount the laps?'"

He hadn't. In fact, he had beaten his own personal
best time by an unbelievable forty-six seconds to
become the first and, as of 2008, only American runner to win the 10,000-meter race.

The history of women's Olympic long-distance
events is much shorter than that of men's. The first
women's 1,500-meter race took place in 1972, the first
5,000-meter race in 1996, and the first 10,000-meter

race in 1988. Of the five 10,000-meter races run, perhaps the most heartwarming was that of the 1992 Barcelona Olympics.

That year marked South Africa's return to the Games. The nation had been banned by the IOC since 1964 because of its system of legal racial segregation known as apartheid. When the laws of apartheid were finally lifted in 1991, South Africa was invited to compete in the next Olympics.

In the starting blocks for the women's 10,000-meter run was the reigning world champion, Elizabeth McColgan of Great Britain, and her chief rival, Ethiopian Derartu Tulu. Also there was Elana Meyer of South Africa.

At the sound of the gun, they and the rest of the pack took off. As expected, McColgan took and held the lead. But after the halfway point, Meyer made a move from the outside lane. McColgan, apparently tiring, didn't put up a fight as Meyer ran past her. Eventually, she fell to fourth and then fifth place.

Meyer, meanwhile, soon found herself just a few paces ahead of Tulu. Lap after lap, they ran one-two with Meyer glancing back every so often as if checking to see that Tulu was still there. Then, just shy of the thirty-minute mark, Tulu lengthened her stride and quickened her pace and with perfect timing passed Meyer. Meyer did her best to recover, but Tulu proved to be the better runner that day. She broke the tape a full five seconds before Meyer.

But Tulu wasn't finished with Meyer yet. It is tradition for runners to take a victory lap after their event. That year, Tulu, who is black, embraced Meyer, who is white, and together the two trotted around the oval, draped in their countries' flags, creating an enduring image of racial unity.

★ CHAPTER SIX ★

Decathlon and Heptathlon

The modern Olympic decathlon is a men's only, ten-event competition that takes place over two days' time. The 100-meter dash, the long jump, the shot put, the high jump, and the 400-meter dash are contested on day one, with the 110-meter hurdles, the discus throw, the pole vault, the javelin, and the 1,500-meter run following the next day. Athletes are awarded points for each event. At the end of the two days, the athlete with the greatest number of points is declared the winner.

The first great decathlon champion was a twenty-four-year-old Native American named Jim Thorpe. Thorpe, a superb college football player and track and field athlete, was already well known in the United States before the 1912 Olympics in Stockholm, Sweden. After the Games, he was a bona fide superstar.

The decathlon wasn't the only event Thorpe entered in 1912. First was the pentathlon, an event discontinued after 1924. This one-day competition consisted of the standing long jump, the javelin, the 200-meter dash, the discus throw, and the 1,500-meter run. Thorpe earned his first gold medal by coming in first place in all but the javelin—which wasn't surprising considering he'd picked up his first javelin just two months before the Olympics. After the pentathlon, he competed in the high jump, where he tied for fourth, and the long jump, where he placed seventh.

Those contests, it turned out, were mere warm-ups for the decathlon. Over the course of two days, Thorpe out-ran, out-threw, and out-jumped nearly every other athlete in the competition to achieve a world-record point total of 8,412.[3] Thorpe's Olympic performances in the decathlon and pentathlon were so impressive that Sweden's King Gustav V publicly congratulated him for being "the greatest athlete in the world." Thorpe's famous reply to that statement was a simple "Thanks, King."

Sadly, less than a year after the Olympics, Thorpe

---

[3] By today's reckoning, that number would be 6,564 because the IOC changed the point allowances in 1985.

was stripped of his medals. The IOC had learned that he had once been paid twenty-five dollars for playing baseball. Although that sum was small, it technically changed his status from amateur to professional athlete. Because the Olympics then were open to amateurs only, he was forced to return his medals and see his name stricken from the books.

While Thorpe admitted to the payment, he argued that the punishment was unfair because the IOC was disregarding its own rule. That rule stated that concerns about an athlete's eligibility had to be registered within thirty days of the end of the Olympics. The IOC didn't take action against him until six months after the 1912 Games. Therefore, Thorpe said, he shouldn't have had his medals taken away.

Thorpe's protests and those of his family and fans were largely ignored until 1982, when the IOC finally reversed its decision. Nearly thirty years after Thorpe's death, duplicates of his medals were presented to his family, and at a long last, his name rejoined the ranks of champions in the Olympic record books.

By that time, several other champions had made it into those same books. Among them was the decathlon's first back-to-back gold medalist and youngest track and field event winner, Bob Mathias. The seventeen-year-old had trained for the decathlon for only four months before going to the 1948 London Games. His inexperience showed at times during the competition. In the shot put, for example, he stepped out of the circle on his first attempt because no one had ever told him he had to stay within it.

Still, after the first day's events, Mathias was in third place. The second day proved difficult for all the athletes because of driving rain and cold temperatures. The track and field areas turned into swamps, causing long delays. Mathias spent much of the wait between events huddled underneath a blanket. But when he emerged, he performed wonderfully.

He completed the 110-meter hurdles in 15.7 seconds, good enough to maintain his third-place rank. He then threw the discus farther than anyone else to jump into first. There was a bit of controversy about that throw, for wind blew down his marker. After much searching for the original scuff mark, he accepted a judgment of 44 meters (144.4 feet) rather than argue for the slightly longer distance he believed he had thrown.

The javelin proved interesting, too. Because of the rain delays, the field was dark by the time the event was held. There were no lights for the field, so cars drove in and turned their headlights onto the foul line. Despite a less-than-stellar throw, Mathias held on to his top rank. And when he crossed the finish line of the 1,500-meter run at 10:35 that night — twelve hours after that day's competition had begun — he became the new decathlon champ.

The next day, after a good night's sleep and the medal ceremony, Mathias told reporters how he planned to celebrate. "I'll start shaving, I guess," he quipped.

Four years later, Mathias won his second Olympic decathlon at the 1952 Helsinki Games. Amazingly, he improved in all ten categories to beat his second-place opponent by nearly one thousand points, the greatest margin ever. He also held the honor of being the only athlete to win two consecutive decathlons until Frances "Daley" Thompson of Great Britain took gold in 1980 in Moscow, Soviet Union, and 1984 in Los Angeles.

The 1984 Los Angeles Games introduced an expanded multievent competition to the women's Olympic program. Since 1960, challengers had tested their skills in the pentathlon, earning points in the 80-meter hurdles, the shot put, the high jump, the long jump, and the 200-meter dash. In 1984, that format was replaced by the seven-category heptathlon. Like the men's decathlon, this endurance event took place over two days, with the 100-meter hurdles, the high jump, the shot put, and the 200-meter dash contested on the first day and the long jump, the javelin, and the 800-meter run on the second.

At the end of the first day of the inaugural Olympic heptathlon, Judith Simpson of Great Britain had the lead. But after the javelin on day two, Simpson had fallen down in the ranks as another athlete rose to the top. That athlete was American Jackie Joyner.

Joyner was on the brink of gold when she lined up for the final event, the 800-meter run. But the first-place medal eluded her that year. Australian Glynis Nunn crossed the finish line ahead of her and wound up winning with a point total of 6,390. Joyner's total was just five points fewer. Had she jumped a mere three centimeters farther in the long jump, she would have won.

That knowledge may have provided the inspiration Joyner (now Jackie Joyner-Kersee after her marriage to her coach, Bob Kersee) needed in her next Olympic heptathlon attempt. She entered the 1988 Seoul Olympics as the clear favorite, having won nine of nine heptathlons since her second-place finish in

1984. She earned more than seven thousand points in four of those victories, silencing critics who said no woman would ever reach that mark and leading *Sports Illustrated* magazine to name her Super Woman.

In Seoul, she held the lead after the first event, the 100-meter hurdles. But she had a setback when, during the high jump, she strained her left knee.

"I was scared," she admitted later. "I was afraid my leg might stiffen."

Her fears were unwarranted. While the strain was undoubtedly painful, it didn't seem to affect her performance greatly. In fact, Joyner-Kersee beat her competition in four of the remaining six categories to set a world record in the heptathlon with 7,291 points. That record still stands as of 2008.

Joyner-Kersee posted another record that same Olympics in the long jump, but it was in the following Games that she made history. Returning as the champion heptathlete, she again bested the competition across the board to win her second gold medal in that category by more than two hundred points. Her score of 7,044 points was the sixth-highest in the world. The five above it were all held by the same person—and that person was Jackie Joyner-Kersee.

1936 Berlin: Jesse Owens is a study in determination and focus as he takes off in the 200-meter dash. The world's fastest man at the time, Owens won four gold medals that year.

1948 London: Seventeen-year-old decathlete Bob Mathias prepares to throw the discus. He captured the gold medal to become one of the youngest Olympic track and field medalists. He repeated as champion in 1952.

1960 Rome: Dawn Fraser (center) made history by taking gold in the 100-meter freestyle race three times in a row, in 1956, 1960, and 1964.

1968 Mexico City: Sprinters Tommie Smith (center) and John Carlos raise clenched fists during the medal ceremony for the 200-meter dash. Their gesture, an enduring image of solidarity, was in silent protest of discrimination against African Americans.

1976 Montreal: It's a perfect 10! Nadia Comaneci performs her dismount in the first flawless uneven-bars routine ever.

1988 Seoul: Flo Jo! Florence Griffith Joyner sprints to the finish line in the 200-meter dash.

1996 Atlanta: Kerri Strug landed hard and injured her left ankle at the end of her first vault routine. She bravely vaulted again and helped the United States earn the team gold.

2008 Beijing: The number-one Olympic athlete in history, Michael Phelps, swims in the qualifier for the 400-meter individual medley. He went on to take the gold medal in that event and seven others, breaking Mark Spitz's record of seven gold medals won in a single Olympics!

Sadly, Joyner-Kersee was forced to pull out of the 1996 heptathlon because of a hamstring injury. Had she been able to compete, she might very well have won, for the total points earned by Ghada Shouaa of Syria, the eventual gold medalist, was 264 points fewer than Joyner-Kersee had made the previous Olympics.

Such an amazing display of athleticism year after year came with one downside. Joyner-Kersee, along with other superior athletes, was suspected of taking performance-enhancing drugs. Many of those others, including the 1992 silver medalist in the heptathlon, failed tests.

Joyner-Kersee never did, proving she was Super Woman indeed.

⋆ CHAPTER SEVEN ⋆
Women's Gymnastics

Gymnastics have been part of the modern Olympics since the first Games in 1896, although it wasn't until 1928 that the first women's event, the team combined exercises, made the program. The team from the Netherlands won that year by a margin of more than twenty-five points.

Like all women's Olympic categories, gymnastics has grown and changed considerably since that time. Nowadays, the athletes compete in four events — the floor exercise program, the uneven bars, the side horse vault, and the balance beam. Each event demands incredible strength, endurance, agility, grace, balance, and mental focus, which is why this Olympic category and its competitors are consistently among the most popular on the program.

The first and arguably greatest female gymnast was

Larisa Latynina of the Soviet Union. She was twenty-one years old when she leaped, spun, flipped, and danced her way to a bronze, a silver, and four gold medals at the 1956 Melbourne Games.

One of those golds was for her floor routine. Grainy black-and-white film of the performance captured her poise and grace, but compared with what female gymnasts do today, the moves themselves don't look particularly challenging—until one considers that she and her fellow competitors were doing them on a surface of carpeted concrete, not springboard!

Over the next eight years, Latynina added twelve more medals, with at least one for each gymnastics category, for a career total of eighteen—nine golds, five silvers, and four bronzes. To this day, Latynina remains the most decorated Olympian, male or female, in history. Her name is also on the very short list of six athletes who have won nine or more gold medals; she is currently the only woman on that list. She holds the record for most medals in individual events, with fourteen. And with the top prize in the floor exercise in 1956, 1960, and 1964, she is one of the few women in any discipline to win gold in the same event three times in a row.

Eight years after Latynina won her final medals, a

new Soviet gymnast took center stage. Petite seventeen-year-old Olga Korbut became the darling of the 1972 Games in Munich, West Germany, when she dazzled judges and spectators with her megawatt smile and her daring moves.

Korbut competed in all four gymnastics categories in each of the three events: the team combined, individual all-around, and individual apparatus. She was talented in all, but it was her performance on the uneven bars that first captivated the audience. A few moments into her routine, she stood briefly on the top bar. Then she let go, backflipped into the air, and grabbed hold of the same bar with her hands!

"Has that been done before by a girl?" one dumbfounded announcer asked another.

"Never! Never!" the second announcer replied excitedly. "Not by any *human* that I know of!"

Korbut's uneven-bars performance helped the Soviets capture the gold medal in the team combined. But unfortunately, that routine didn't go as smoothly for her during the all-around competition. First, her feet caught on the mat during her initial mount, forcing her to begin again. Later, her hands slipped. Toward the end, she lost momentum during a swing on the upper bar.

"And she's lost it there. The gold medal [for all-around], I'm certain, has gone," an announcer sadly declared.

The crowd was silent as Korbut finished the routine and hurried to the sidelines. Then, with the television cameras trained on her and a lowly 7.5 showing on the scoreboard, she broke down weeping. She finished the event in seventh place.

But the gymnastics competition wasn't over yet. Still to come were the individual apparatus events. And here, Korbut shone.

In the floor exercise, she delighted the audience with her graceful display of athleticism as well as the look of pure enjoyment radiating from her pixielike face. The judges liked what they saw, too, especially in her second routine. They awarded her a score of 9.9 for that performance—and the gold medal.

She earned gold for the balance beam, too, thanks to a spectacular effort in the second round. She received a 9.5 for her first performance. That put her just slightly behind teammate Tamara Lazakovich. To beat Lazakovich for the gold medal, Korbut needed a 9.9.

She got it, with moves few people had seen before. Midway through the routine, she flipped backward on the four-inch-wide bar, landing softly on her hands and then dropping down into a gentle but elegant chest roll.

"To dive blindly like that backwards," a commentator said later, "that took nerve."

And Korbut wasn't done yet. At the end of her routine, she leaped high above the bar, tucked into a ball, spun backward in a somersault, and landed back on the beam without the slightest wobble. As the crowd erupted into cheers and applause, she flipped forward and off, sticking her dismount before breaking into a wide, beaming smile and waving with both hands. Her score was 9.9, and the gold medal was hers!

Korbut came close to earning another gold for the uneven bars. Instead, she tied for silver—despite a prolonged and very vocal protest from the spectators, who believed she deserved better than the 9.8 she received from the judges. The judges stood firm, however. Korbut and her many fans had to be content with the tie.

Korbut finished with three golds and one silver. But more important than her medal count was the impact she had on the sport itself. With her seemingly impossible moves, she raised the bar for gymnasts everywhere. She also opened the door for younger girls to compete at the highest level.

Korbut would compete against—and lose to—one of those younger girls in the 1976 Games in Montreal, Canada. Romanian Nadia Comaneci was just fourteen years old when she performed a stunning balance-beam routine during the team competition. From the moment she mounted the skinny bar to when she returned to the mat, her movements seemed flawless. But then her score flashed on the screen.

"1.00? Is that a joke?!" spectators must have said to one another when they saw the number.

It wasn't a joke; it was an equipment failure. The scoring machine only had a single space to the left of the decimal point. But Comaneci's score required two spaces because she had just accomplished something no Olympic gymnast ever had: a perfect 10.00!

That perfect score was followed by an unbelievable six more. Comaneci won gold medals in the individual balance-beam and uneven-bars events. She also took gold in the individual all-around, the first Romanian to win that prize. In fact, Comaneci was the first Romanian athlete, male or female, to win a gold medal in gymnastics. She had a silver and a bronze, too, for team competition and floor exercise.

Comaneci repeated as the individual balance-beam

champion and added a fifth career gold medal with a win in the floor exercise at the 1980 Moscow Games. She just narrowly missed capturing the all-around title again. Going into her second balance-beam routine, she needed a 9.9 to tie for first. But after deliberating for nearly half an hour, the judges awarded her 9.85. So instead, a silver medal hung around her neck for all-around.

Comaneci didn't compete in another Olympics, but nine years after the Moscow Games, she made headlines again. That's when the public learned she had defected from Romania, a Communist nation, to live in the United States. Escaping her homeland was very dangerous but worth it, she said. "I like life. I want to live a free life."

Comaneci, Korbut, Latynina: The early decades of women's Olympic gymnastics had been dominated by athletes from Soviet and Eastern European nations. In comparison, the United States had earned just a single medal, a bronze in 1948 for team combined. In 1984, however, the Americans finally added one of their own to the list of champions.

Sixteen-year-old Mary Lou Retton fit the profile of a star gymnast to a T. She was small in stature, but her tiny frame was made of sheer muscle. She had trained for years before reaching the Olympics. She had grace, athleticism—and a wide, winning smile that brought back memories of Olga Korbut.

Retton was one of thirty-six gymnasts to take part in the all-around competition that year. Going into the final round, she had a score of 39.525. That gave her a slight edge over the much-favored Romanian, Ecaterina Szabo, who had 39.375. Then Szabo gave an amazing performance on the balance beam that earned her a perfect 10. Retton, meanwhile, was given a score of 9.85 for her uneven-bars routine.

The two were now tied for first place. Retton dropped behind by fifteen one-hundredths of a point when Szabo earned a near-perfect score of 9.95 for her floor exercise; Retton, performing on the balance beam, received 9.8. Retton fought back, however, with a dramatic and seamless floor routine that the judges awarded a 10. She now trailed by less than two-tenths of one point.

Szabo had earned a 9.9 for her vault; her final apparatus was the uneven bars. Again, she was near-perfect. As Retton prepared for her final event, the vault, Szabo's score of 9.9 flashed on the board. To beat Szabo, Retton would need to nail her vault. A 9.95 would tie her with Szabo for the gold; a 10 would put the gold around her neck only.

Retton moved into position at the end of the runway. She got the green light and took off at a dead sprint. She hit the springboard, launched high above the horse, whirled and twisted through the air, and landed without a trace of a wobble!

"She has done the best vault of her life!" the announcer cried. The Los Angeles crowd roared and cheered. Retton bounced and waved, grinning from ear to ear, before throwing herself into her coach's arms for a huge hug.

"I knew by my run that I had it," she told reporters later. "I knew it when I was in the air!"

When the perfect score flashed on the panel, the spectators leaped to their feet with deafening screams. Mary Lou Retton was the all-around Olympic champion! She didn't even need to perform her second vault because the gold medal was hers. She did it anyway, repeating the same layout back somersault with the double twist. Her score? Another perfect 10.

Americans who hoped Retton's success would unleash a wave of top female gymnasts from the United States were no doubt disappointed when the 1988

Seoul Olympics saw a return of the Eastern European and Soviet dominance. But in 1992, they had reason to cheer again. The Barcelona Games featured the strongest U.S. team ever to hit the mats. Shannon Miller, Dominique Dawes, Kerri Strug, and the rest took bronze in the team combined that year; Miller also added silvers in the all-around and balance beam, plus bronzes in the uneven-bars and floor-exercise events.

Many from that talented squad returned to the Olympics again in 1996 — and again, they performed beautifully. Miller nabbed the gold in balance beam. Teammate Amy Chow tied for silver in the uneven bars. Dawes took bronze in the floor exercise. But it was Strug who left the most lasting impression in women's gymnastics that year.

Strug was one of the lesser-known members of the team the press had dubbed the Magnificent Seven. She had all the skill and athleticism the sport demanded, but she was often criticized for buckling under pressure or giving in to the pain that accompanies the sport. On July 23, 1996, those critics saw firsthand just how wrong they were about Strug.

Strug was on the sidelines, watching her teammate Dominique Moceanu prepare to vault as part of the team combined competition. It was a historic moment, for a good score would give Team USA its first gold in that category. But to Strug's horror, her teammate fell not once but twice.

The vault was the last event of the team combined. Strug was the last member of the team to perform. She had to earn at least a 9.6 or risk costing her squad the gold medal.

With perhaps the greatest pressure she'd ever felt weighing on her tiny shoulders, Strug raced down the runway, hit the horse with both hands, and whirled through the air. But when she landed, the unthinkable happened.

"I fell on my first vault and heard a pop in my left ankle," Strug later wrote. "A jolt of pain ran up my leg."

As Strug got gingerly to her feet, television cameras zeroed in on her face. She appeared to be fighting back tears, and when she began limping off the mat, it was obvious something was wrong with her ankle.

She received a low score of 9.162. If the United States was to stay in the lead, Strug had to do her second vault. She had to vault better and, most important, she had to stick the landing.

But with an injured ankle, how could she hope to get down the runway, let alone leap, twirl, and land?

That's when Strug's inner strength took over. She sprinted full speed and did a round off onto the springboard. Rebounding upward, she hit the horse with both hands, pushed off, and twirled with grace and speed. And then, with the eyes of the world upon her, she landed solidly on both feet with only the merest whisper of a bobble. As she raised her hands over her head, the signal that her vault was complete, she also lifted her left foot. And then she crumpled to the floor and dissolved into tears.

Trainers on the U.S. staff quickly helped Strug to the side. Now all that remained was to see if her heroic effort had paid off.

Finally, the number flashed on the board.

"A 9.712! She has done it!" the announcer bellowed.

It later came to light that Strug didn't need to do her second vault after all, for the team had clinched the gold already. But she had needed to do it to advance to the all-around competition. Unfortunately, her ankle injury was too severe to allow her to take part in those events.

Strug's historic vault remains one of the most inspiring Olympic moments of any sport. While the 2000, 2004, and 2008 Games produced champions, including Carly Patterson, the first American all-around winner since Mary Lou Retton, no one yet has come close to the bravery exhibited by that member of the Magnificent Seven.

"I believed in myself and went after my dreams," Strug once wrote.

Those words could have come from any of the thousands of athletes, male or female, from any discipline and from any of the Olympic Games, from far in the past to long into the future. For the strength to be a champion begins with a dream to be the best.

★ CHAPTER EIGHT ★

Men's Gymnastics

As a youngster, George Eyser was nearly killed when he was accidentally run over by a train. He survived, but his left leg was amputated and replaced with a wooden one. If his later athletic accomplishments are any indication, Eyser adjusted to the prosthetic limb without much trouble.

Eyser was the star on the United States men's gymnastics squad at the 1904 Olympics in St. Louis, Missouri. These Games were unusual because the events took place over several months to coincide with the World's Fair. Gymnastics were split into two categories, with half in early July and half in late October.

Eyser didn't do well in July, but in the fall, he crushed his rivals. He took gold in the now discontinued rope-climbing event, shimmying up the twenty-five-foot length in 7 seconds flat. He tied for gold in the long horse vault. Considering they didn't use a springboard in those days, this was somewhat miraculous for a man with a wooden leg. He added a third gold for his parallel-bars routine — and then two silvers and a bronze for a single-day total of six medals!

Men's gymnastics events and equipment haven't changed much since Eyser's day. Competition is divided into three categories, the team combined, the individual all-around, and the individual events, and it takes place on six apparatuses: the high bar, parallel bars, rings, pommel horse, long horse vault, and floor exercise.

Of the three categories, a gold in the individual all-around is the most coveted. In 1908 and 1912, Alberto Braglia of Italy became the first gymnast in Olympic history to repeat as champion in the category.

Forty years later, Viktor Ivanovich Chukarin won his first all-around. Chukarin was born in Ukraine in 1921. A budding gymnast, he swapped his athletic career to become a soldier when World War II broke out. Not long after he joined, he was imprisoned in a German concentration camp for four years. He survived to return home in 1945.

Chukarin resumed training and by 1948 was the dominant gymnast of the new Soviet Union. He didn't compete in the London Games, however. The Soviet Union did not participate, and Japan and Germany had been banned as punishment for their part in the war.

They were all back for the 1952 Helsinki Games, and there, Chukarin rolled over his competition. He won the individual all-around, the pommel horse, and the vault, and he helped the Soviet Union win its first team combined gold medal. He also took silvers in the rings and parallel bars.

At age thirty-five, Chukarin won his second all-around gold at the 1956 Melbourne Games. He added golds in team combined and parallel bars, a silver in floor exercise, and a bronze in pommel horse to finish his Olympic career with a then record total of eleven medals.

If Chukarin was the king of the Melbourne Games, then Takashi Ono of Japan was his prince. In addition to a silver medal in the all-around, Ono won the horizontal bar event to become the first Japanese gymnast to earn an individual gold medal. He took second in the pommel horse and team competition, plus a bronze for the parallel bars.

When Chukarin's reign ended after the 1956 Games, Ono picked up the crown. He participated in two more Olympics, and in 1964, he surpassed Chukarin with a final tally of thirteen medals: five golds, four silvers, and four bronzes.

Ono bowed out of the next Olympics, but in his place rose another dynamic Japanese gymnast. Sawao Kato had been training since his early teens. In 1968, that training paid off.

In the individual all-around competition, he was trailing Soviet Mikhail Voronin when he took to the mat for his floor-exercise routine. He needed a 9.85 to tie for the gold. His performance was a near-perfect exhibition of athleticism, style, grace, and strength. He reached incredible heights in his aerial moves, held poses without a wobble, and stuck his landings with precision. When his score of 9.9 hit the monitor, the crowd and announcers erupted with cheers for Kato, the new all-around champion.

Four years later, Kato became the third gymnast to defend his individual all-around title. While he missed adding a historic third in 1976, he did take golds in the team combined and parallel bars. In all, he collected twelve medals — eight golds, three silvers, and one bronze — to end his Olympic career as one of the top gymnasts of all time.

His teammate Shun Fujimoto was not as successful, but at the 1976 Games, Fujimoto earned a place in people's hearts for his determination and bravery. Japan was neck-and-neck with the Soviets for the team combined gold when Fujimoto performed his floor routine. But during his last tumbling run, something went wrong with his right knee.

"It felt hollow," he said later, "as if there were air in it."

That hollow feeling was soon replaced by something else: severe pain. Fujimoto had broken his kneecap. The injury should have sent him to the sidelines for good. Instead, Fujimoto hid his pain and continued on to his next event, the pommel horse. There, though he was in agony, he gave one of his best performances, earning a 9.5 for his team.

Fujimoto's final routine was the rings. Drawing on inner strength, he turned in a career-best, near-flawless performance that ended with a twisting triple-somersault dismount. He landed solidly on both feet and raised his arms to signal the completion of his routine — despite a bolt of pain that shot through his leg.

"How he managed to do somersaults and twists and land without collapsing in screams," marveled one doctor later, "is beyond my comprehension."

Years later, Fujimoto admitted that it was beyond his comprehension, too. When asked if he'd do now what he'd done then, he gave a very straightforward answer: "No."

Fujimoto's heroic effort gave the Japanese team the boost they needed to win their fifth consecutive team combined gold medal. It was one of the tightest wins in Olympic history, 576.85 points to the Soviet Union's 576.45.

Japan didn't get a chance to defend its title at the 1980 Moscow Olympics, for they joined a U.S.-led boycott to protest the Soviet Union's recent invasion of Afghanistan. The boycott hoped to draw attention to the Soviet Union, which would not withdraw its troops. Unfortunately, the athletes of the sixty-five boycotting nations, not the Soviet forces, ultimately paid the price when their years of training—and dreaming—ended up being for nothing.

Not surprisingly, the Soviets rose to the top of the medal charts in 1980. They claimed 195 in all, including eighty gold medals, five of which were won by their men's gymnastics team. At the head of that team were two extraordinary athletes, Nikolai Andrianov and Aleksandr Dityatin.

It was Andrianov's third trip to the Olympics. He

won his first gold medal in 1972 for his floor-exercise routine. In 1976, he unseated Kato in the individual all-around competition. He repeated as the champion in floor exercise and took golds in the rings and vault, too. In 1980, he captured another gold for vault and was a critical part in winning the team combined competition. In all, he garnered fifteen medals in his Olympic career—the most of any male athlete in the world until 2008.

Equally impressive was the medal count racked up by Dityatin. Five years younger than Andrianov, Dityatin stood in his teammate's shadow for much of his career. In 1980, however, he surpassed his elder by winning medals in all eight gymnastic categories, the first gymnast to accomplish such a feat. Three of those medals were gold, including the coveted all-around. In that competition, his most spectacular moment came during his long horse vault. That's when he earned the first perfect 10 score ever awarded to a male gymnast.

Sadly, the 1980 Moscow Games would be the last Olympics for Dityatin and Andrianov. Andrianov retired soon afterward. Dityatin might have taken part in the 1984 Los Angeles competition, but he was badly injured during training in late 1980. Even if he had been healthy, he couldn't have competed, for the Soviet Union retaliated for the 1980 boycott by sitting out the 1984 Games.

The Soviets' absence in Los Angeles opened an opportunity for a team that had up until this time underperformed. The United States' athletes were strong in many Olympic categories but not in gymnastics. In 1984, however, the nation had its first gold medal–winning team in more than fifty years.

On the squad were Olympic newcomers Timothy Daggett, Mitch Gaylord, and Scott Johnson, as well as James Hartung, Peter Vidmar, and Bart Conner, veterans of earlier Games.

The team's biggest challenge was China. Going into the competition, that nation was the odds-on favorite to take the gold medal in the team combined as well as several other events.

But that's not quite how it turned out.

The team combined took place over two days. After the first day, the United States was in the lead with a commanding 1.05 advantage over China!

The second day saw teams competing in the optional category, where the athletes performed original routines. It was here that the United States' gymnasts shone.

During the team combined, different events run at the same time. First up for the Americans was the floor exercise; the Chinese, meanwhile, performed their side horse routines. All six Americans performed well and so held their lead. But the Chinese weren't finished yet. On their next rotation, the rings, they earned two perfect 10s to edge closer to their rivals, whose scores for the pommel horse were sound but not stellar.

When it was the United States' turn on the parallel bars, Mitch Gaylord turned in a historic performance. With amazing power and control, he muscled his way to his team's first perfect 10.

The U.S. team retained a slim lead. But then the six Chinese gymnasts earned 9.9 or higher on the parallel bars. The Americans' lead grew even slimmer.

Now it was the United States' turn on the bars. Bart Conner mounted the apparatus from the side and whipped up and around into back-to-back handstands. Then he dropped into a split-legged pike and rotated hand-over-hand before slowly rising up into a single-bar handstand. He finished the routine with a somersaulting dismount for a score of 9.9.

The Americans were now one step closer to the gold medal. But once again, the Chinese blocked their path with magnificent performances, this time on the high bar. With just one rotation left to go, China trailed by a little more than half a point.

Now the Chinese took to the mats for the floor exercise while the Americans went to the high bar. The Chinese were phenomenal, posting scores of 9.9 or better. If the U.S. team was to hold its lead, none of its athletes could make a mistake.

Of the routines, Gaylord's was the riskiest. It included a move that is named after him, the Gaylord II, in which he lets go of the bar, soars over the top in a twisting somersault, and then grabs hold again. He missed the move as often as he made it. This time, he nailed it perfectly to earn a score of 9.95.

Inspired by his teammate, Tim Daggett scored the squad's third perfect 10 with his own high bar routine. That score clinched the title for the Americans.

The arena erupted in cheers. So did the American gymnasts. "I suddenly got very, very light-headed and almost passed out," Vidmar remembered. "I think it was from all the shouting and yelling we were doing. I got real dizzy, but then I figured, so what if I pass out? I've still got this medal around my neck."

More medals followed. Conner took home gold

with another outstanding parallel bars routine. Vidmar narrowly missed the gold in the all-around and tied for first with Li Ning of China in the pommel horse. Gaylord was one of four silver medalists in the vault, and a bronze medal winner in the parallel bars and rings. Daggett also nabbed a bronze, for the pommel.

The U.S. triumph raised hopes for future victories in men's gymnastics. But unfortunately, those hopes were dashed in the following Olympics. After missing out in 1984, the Soviets returned in full force in 1988. Led by Vladimir Artemov, they won six and tied once out of eight possible gold medals. The United States won none.

Between the 1988 Seoul and the 1992 Barcelona Games, world politics underwent a major change. The once-powerful Soviet Union collapsed in December 1991. After that collapse, several former Soviet countries declared independence and began the long and difficult transition to economic and political sovereignty.

With the Olympics coming so soon after the start of that transition, twelve fledgling nations agreed to field a joint squad, dubbed the Unified Team. The star of the Unified men's gymnastics team was Vitaly

Scherbo of Belarus. Scherbo wasn't just good; he was the best gymnast to hit the Olympics ever. He set a record by winning gold medals in six of the eight events, including the all-around title.

And yet unlike other champions, the stern-faced Scherbo didn't win the hearts of the public. His routines were seen as mechanical rather than inspired. Scherbo ignored the criticism and set his sights on the 1996 Games in Atlanta, Georgia.

Tragic events almost derailed those plans. In December 1995, his wife, Irina, was in a near-fatal car crash that left her in a coma for weeks. Scherbo stayed by her side almost the entire time—but during his vigil, he drank so much alcohol that his friend Alexander Kolyvanov, a former Soviet gymnast, scarcely recognized him.

Kolyvanov insisted that Scherbo start taking care of himself. Scherbo listened, and when Irina awoke from her coma a month later, he was ready to take care of her, too. He also began training for the Atlanta Games again. Although time away had certainly taken its toll, he still performed well enough to earn four bronzes.

And yet he was applauded more enthusiastically for those bronzes than he had been when he had won gold four years earlier, for the audience knew of his hardships. Their applause was as much for his bravery as it was for his talent.

In 2004, a comeback of a different sort had the crowd cheering. American gymnast Paul Hamm was in contention for a medal in the all-around competition when he stepped up to perform his vault. But to the audience's horror, Hamm finished his twisting somersault in a half crouch and, off-balance, stumbled sideways right into the judges' table. His dismal score of 9.137 sent him plummeting into twelfth place.

"I was very upset and depressed," he admitted. "I felt I let myself down."

A medal seemed out of reach. But then fate took over, as other gymnasts made costly mistakes that knocked them out of contention.

Suddenly in fourth place, Hamm gave his absolute best in his final two routines, the parallel bars and high bar. That best, it turned out, was good enough for gold, the first time an American male gymnast had claimed that medal in the all-around.

But had he really won? The bronze medalist, South Korean Yang Tae Young, didn't think so. The South Korean team filed a complaint saying he had been incorrectly docked a fraction of a point on one of his routines. If the governing authority, the Court of Arbitration for Sports (CAS), agreed with Young, then he, not Hamm, would be the gold medalist.

After hearing arguments from both sides, the CAS ruled that the rankings would stand as they were, with Hamm in first and Young in third.

No one knows what the future holds for gymnastics, but one thing is certain: All gymnasts deserve the public's admiration for their dedication to their sport, their teams, and their craft.

☆ CHAPTER NINE ☆
Women's Swimming

Women's swimming first appeared on the Olympic program in 1912. The category was slow to grow, with just two races at those Stockholm Games and only three in the 1920 Antwerp Games. (The Olympics were canceled in 1916 because of World War I.) Those three events, the 100-meter, 300-meter (later 400-meter), and 4×100-meter, were all freestyle events—and all three were won by the same swimmer, eighteen-year-old American Ethelda Bleibtrey, who set or helped set world records in each. Had backstroke been offered, she would probably have emerged as the first swimmer to win four gold medals in a single Olympics, for she held the world record in that event at the time. As it was, she earned her place in Olympic history as the first woman to win three top prizes.

Outside of the Olympics, Bleibtrey was something of a rebel. She was once given a summons for swimming at a public beach without her stockings, an act akin to swimming nude in the eyes of the law back then. She was arrested again a few years later while protesting the lack of swimming pools in New York City.

Bleibtrey had long retired from swimming—and rebelling—by the time the next female Olympic swimming champion arrived on the scene. Australian Dawn Fraser competed in her first Games in 1956 in Melbourne. There she set a world record in the 100-meter freestyle with a time of 1:02. She also took home gold for the freestyle relay and silver for the 400-meter freestyle.

Fraser won the 100-meter freestyle title at the 1960 Rome Games, making her the first woman to defend her Olympic swimming title. She added a silver for the 4×100-meter medley relay, too, despite nearly sitting out the race because of an altercation with her teammates.

The trouble started brewing the day after Fraser's historic 100-meter freestyle win. Her teammates and coach expected her to swim the butterfly leg of the

4×100-meter medley relay qualifier. But when race time came, she refused to swim, claiming she was too full from a recent pasta meal. Although she eventually swam in the final as the anchor, her attitude so angered her teammates that they gave her the cold shoulder for the rest of the Games.

Fraser was back at the Olympics in 1964. Her presence there was something of a miracle. Just a year earlier, she had been in a terrible car accident that claimed her mother's life and left Fraser and her sister badly injured. Through determination and hard work, Fraser returned to form and in Tokyo did what no swimmer, male or female, had then or has yet to do again: She won the same event, the 100-meter freestyle race, for a third consecutive time.

Unfortunately, Fraser also displayed a complete lack of judgment while in Tokyo. Before the Games began, she defied orders from the Australian Swimming Union and marched in the opening ceremony. Then she chose not to wear the official swimsuit during her gold medal–winning race, which angered her sponsor, swimsuit maker Speedo. Finally, the night after her victory, she stole an Olympic flag from outside the Imperial Palace. As punishment for her actions, Fraser was banned from all competitive swimming for the next ten years. While the ban was eventually reduced to four years, Fraser's career was over.

The 100-meter freestyle race is the most anticipated event of the swimming program, but it is just one of five individual freestyle events. The other four are the 50-meter, 200-meter, 400-meter, and 800-meter. In 1968, one American swimmer amazed the sporting world by winning gold medals and setting Olympic records in three.

In 1964, twelve-year-old Debbie Meyer received a special Christmas present from her father. It was a stopwatch. The back was engraved with the words *Debbie Meyer: December 25, 1964–Mexico City 1968*. Meyer liked the watch but later remembered thinking the engraving was "the dorkiest thing in the world," for at the time she didn't really know what the Olympics were all about.

She learned all she needed to know in the four years that followed. She made the U.S. team and in early October set off to compete in the 1968 Mexico City Games.

Her first race was the 400-meter freestyle. She touched the wall nearly four seconds ahead of the silver medalist. Next up was the 200-meter race. It was the first time this event was on the women's swimming program. Meyer won it by half a second. Then came the 800-meter race, again offered for the first time that Olympics. Here, Meyer didn't just win; she left the competition wallowing in her wake. She finished in 9:24, or more than eleven seconds ahead of the runner-up!

When Meyer emerged from the pool after winning that third race, she entered the Olympic history books as the first female swimmer to win three gold medals in individual events.

"I look back now," Meyer recalled forty years later, "and I go, 'How did I do that?'"

Meyer's feat was unmatched for the next eight years. Then, in 1976, Kornelia Ender from East Germany topped Meyer by winning four gold medals, three for individual races and one for the 4×100-meter medley relay. In three, she set world records.

Ender's performance that Olympics was so dominating that some believed it would never be beat. Yet just twelve years later, another East German swimmer, Kristin Otto, flashed through the pool lanes in Seoul on her way to an astonishing six gold medals!

While Otto's performance had many people cheering, it also had many eyeing her and other East German medalists with growing suspicion. East Germany had always had a good Olympic program. But since 1968, their medal total had increased dramatically, from twenty-five in Mexico City to 102 in Seoul. Had the number of athletes grown, too, then that increase might have made sense.

But the number was essentially the same, from 226 competitors in 1968 to 259 in 1988. So what was leading to East Germany's sudden domination? The answer seemed obvious: performance-enhancing drugs. Adding weight to those suspicions was the fact that many of the female athletes, among them Ender and Otto, showed signs of using anabolic steroids, including deep, husky voices and unusually muscular builds.

Three years after Otto's victories, the truth came to light. Throughout the 1970s and 1980s, the East German coaches and training staff had given performance-enhancing drugs to their athletes — without the athletes' knowledge or consent.

"I remember being given injections during training and competition," Ender said in a 1991 interview, "but this was explained to me as being substances to help me regenerate and recuperate. ... We were never asked if we wanted it; it was just given."

Otto has never denied that she was also a victim of the program, but she refused to believe her abilities were simply the result of steroids. "I worked very hard for those medals.... It was not all drugs," she insisted.

Because they did not willingly participate in the drug program, none of the East German athletes have had their medals or records stripped by the IOC. Still, many of them may have been left wondering if they truly belong in the Olympic books.

Kristin Otto wasn't the only powerhouse female swimmer in 1988—although to see American Janet Evans standing with the others, one might not think she offered much competition. But she not only beat the field to earn three gold medals, but she also beat them handily.

Her first win came in the 400-meter individual medley. She swam the butterfly lap well, but she really made her move during the backstroke leg. She stayed in front throughout the breaststroke and by the race's freestyle leg, had pulled ahead by a full body length. And when she finished, she was a gold medalist.

As strong as she was in the medley, she was even better in the 400-meter freestyle race. She took the lead early on, but Heike Friedrich of East Germany wasn't far behind. With a hundred meters left to go, Evans was in front by no more than a foot.

Then Evans did something unbelievable: She sped up and completed the race faster than she had started it. When her fingertips brushed the wall at the end, she had beaten her own world record by more than a second and Friedrich by more than two seconds!

It was no contest in the 800-meter freestyle, either. Evans was half a lap ahead of some of the other swimmers for much of the race. Although she didn't beat her own world record, she did set an Olympic record.

Evans returned to the Olympics in 1992 and repeated as the 800-meter freestyle champion. She took silver in the 400-meter freestyle as well. And at the 1996 Atlanta Games, she had the honor of passing the Olympic torch to boxing great and former Olympian Muhammad Ali, who then lit the cauldron's flame.

Another great American swimmer was Dara Torres. She became an Olympic medalist for the first time in 1984, when she won gold as part of the 4×100-meter freestyle team. She added a silver and a bronze to her collection in 1988 and another gold in 1992. She retired from swimming after Barcelona, believing that at twenty-five she was too old to continue competing at such a high level.

But after skipping the 1996 Atlanta Games, she did something that stunned the swimming world: She came back, qualified for the 2000 Olympic team, and won more medals—two golds and three bronzes—than anyone else on the squad! With nine Olympic medals to her credit, Torres pondered retirement again. She sat out the 2004 Games, but she just couldn't stay away from the water.

"I don't like to do anything halfway," she wrote later, "and I'd set this crazy goal for myself: to make my fifth Olympic team as a forty-one-year-old mother." She did qualify, and in 2008 made history as the oldest U.S. swimmer to win a medal—or rather, three medals, all silver, to bring her twenty-four-year Olympic career total to a whopping twelve.

One of those silvers came in the 50-meter freestyle, considered by some to be the most challenging race because of its short duration. Swimmers who fall even slightly behind simply don't have a chance to catch up. Torres was neck-and-neck with the winner, twenty-five-year-old Britta Steffen of Germany, throughout the dash, finishing just .01 seconds after her.

Not surprisingly, Torres's amazing performances led to accusations of doping. Her reaction was swift, sure, and very public.

"Do whatever you want," she told the United States Anti-Doping Agency. "I want to show people I'm clean." Hair, urine, and blood tests all proved she was exactly that. Her skill, not drugs, had won those medals.

On the list of superb female swimmers from the United States, Natalie Coughlin is at the top. How good is she? Torres won twelve medals in five Olympics; Coughlin won eleven—three golds, four silvers, and four bronzes—in just two. Even more impressive, she has medaled in every Olympic event she's ever entered!

Coughlin's first medal of the 2004 Athens Games was silver. She earned it by swimming the second leg in the 4×100-meter freestyle relay.

Her second race was also her best event, the 100-meter backstroke. She lined up in the water, facing the wall and gripping the bar of the diving podium. When the gun went off, she hurled herself backward and plunged beneath the surface. Face up and arms straight overhead, she dolphin-kicked forcefully, propelling herself ahead of the others. When she came up for air, she had the lead. That lead increased after her turn. When she touched the wall after the second length, she had her first gold medal.

Two days later, she was the leadoff swimmer for the 4×200-meter freestyle relay. She was so strong that had she been swimming the individual 200-meter freestyle event, she most likely would have won easily. As it was, she and her teammates set a world record of 7:53.42. She finished the Games with a bronze in the 100-meter freestyle and a silver in the 4×100-meter medley relay. In this second race, she swam the backstroke leg—and set a world record by covering her one hundred meters in 59.68 seconds.

The Olympics in Beijing saw Coughlin doing what no other female swimmer had ever done, namely repeating as the 100-meter backstroke champion. That was her only gold of the Games, but with the three bronzes and two silvers she earned in the days that followed, she left as the only American woman to ever earn six medals at a single Olympics.

✴ CHAPTER TEN ✴

Men's Swimming

Swimming events have been part of the modern-day Olympics since the 1896 Athens Games, although the events themselves have changed and expanded considerably. In the early Olympics, they were held in open water, regardless of the chop or water temperature. The water was so cold in 1896 that the winner of the 100-meter freestyle race, Alfred Hajos of Hungary, later admitted, "My will to live completely overcame my desire to win."

The first Games featured mainly freestyle and breaststroke races. The backstroke was added in 1904 and the butterfly in 1956.

Besides the races, the earliest Olympic Games had a few oddball aquatic competitions. The 1900 Paris Games, for example, included an underwater swim for distance and a 200-meter obstacle course that saw athletes climbing over a pole in the water and swimming around and under boats. Four years later, divers took part in a plunge-for-distance event in which they dove into a pool and then stayed underwater for as long as they could without moving. After their initial appearances, none of these three events ever found their way back onto the Olympic program.

Races first moved to specially built pools at the 1908 London Games. The signature event, the 100-meter freestyle, was won by an American named Charles Daniels. Daniels was one of the first great swimmers from the United States, earning a total of four golds, one silver, and two bronzes in the 1904 and 1908 Games. He is also credited with improving the crawl stroke by developing the six-beat kick, a rhythm that is still widely used today.

The next big name in men's swimming was indeed a "big" name: Duke Paoa Kahinu Mokoe Hulikohola Kahanamoku. A native of Hawaii, Kahanamoku took golds in the 100-meter events in 1912 and 1920, setting a world record in the latter race, and then added a silver in the same category in 1924. He also won a third gold and a second silver, both for the 4×200-meter freestyle relay.

A popular figure who later appeared in several

movies and television shows, Kahanamoku spent time after the Olympics promoting his other favorite sport, surfing. Few people outside Hawaii knew much about surfing until Kahanamoku gave demonstrations while touring the world after his Olympic victories. He demonstrated the surfboard's practical purpose, too, when he used it to rescue several passengers from a capsized ship off the coast of California.

The swimmer who beat Kahanamoku in the 1924 100-meter freestyle race would himself go on to international fame, not just as a champion but as a movie star. In 1922, Johnny Weissmuller was the first man to swim a hundred meters in less than a minute; two years later, he won gold by swimming that distance in 59 seconds, an Olympic record. He set another record in the 400-meter freestyle event to earn his second gold — and added a third plus a world record as the anchor for the 4×200-meter freestyle relay team and a bronze as a member of the water polo team.

Four years later, he defended his 100-meter championship, beating his own time by four-tenths of a second — despite nearly losing consciousness after taking in a huge mouthful of water midway through the race. He finished the 1928 Games with another gold and a world record in the 4×200-meter relay.

Weissmuller planned to enter the 1932 Olympics but instead accepted a profitable job modeling swimsuits. That job led to a career playing Tarzan the Ape Man in the movies. Interestingly, three other Olympic athletes, Clarence "Buster" Crabbe, Herman Brix, and Glenn Morris, would also play that role.

The United States continued to perform well across the board in men's swimming in the years that followed. But until 1964, no one man stood out above the rest. Then Don Schollander appeared on the scene.

Too small to play high school football as he'd hoped, Schollander switched to swimming his freshman year. By his senior year, he was setting world records, winning national championships, and training for the Olympics. He made the U.S. team easily and then proceeded to demolish the competition at the 1964 Tokyo Games. He entered four events — the 100-meter freestyle, the 400-meter freestyle, the first-ever 4×100-meter freestyle relay, and the 4×200-meter freestyle relay — and won gold medals in all four. No other swimmer from any other country had ever won that many in a single Olympics.

When the eighteen-year-old Schollander returned home to Oregon, he was hailed as a hero. "I had expected to see just my parents," he remembered years later. Instead, he was greeted by a sea of fans, the press, and his high school band. While some people would have welcomed such attention, Schollander hated it. In fact, he wanted nothing more than to be left in peace.

Fortunately for Schollander, there was a new swimmer on the horizon who would soon overshadow his accomplishments. Schollander trained with him for the 1968 Mexico City Games, and together they helped their 4×200 team win the gold medal.

That swimmer's name? Mark Spitz.

Spitz took to the water very early in his life. "You should have seen that little boy dash into the ocean," his mother laughingly recalled of her son's love of the sea.

When he was old enough, Spitz began swimming competitively. By the time he was ten, he had set his first national record. As a teenager, he continued to win and set records.

Like many great athletes, Spitz was blessed with a body built for his chosen sport. His hands were large, which helped him scoop and push more water for greater power. His knees had a little extra flex that allowed him to get more thrust out of every kick. By his calculation, he needed thirteen strokes to get from one end of the pool to the other, while other swimmers typically needed fifteen or more.

Spitz also had the mental toughness it took to train for the Olympics. By 1968, he was so confident in his ability that he publicly predicted that he'd win six gold medals in Mexico City. He fell short of that goal by four, but he used his failure to spur himself on to train even harder for the 1972 Munich Games.

Spitz had shown great promise in 1968, but in 1972, he positively shone. Even before the Olympics began, he was a celebrity in Germany, recognizable thanks to his mustache — a rarity among male swimmers, many of whom believed facial hair slowed them down in the water. If that was true, it didn't affect Spitz one bit.

He entered four individual races and three team relays. First up was the 200-meter butterfly. Introduced to the Games in 1956, the butterfly is the most physically challenging of the four Olympic strokes. It requires tremendous shoulder strength and perfect timing on kicks. Spitz proved he had both, winning the race with a world-record time of 2:00.7. He was so elated with the victory that after he touched the wall, he leaped for joy.

That same day, Spitz swam anchor in the 4×400-meter freestyle relay. He and his teammates, David Edgar, John Murphy, and Jerry Heidenreich, beat the second-place team by more than three seconds and set a world record.

Spitz continued his winning streak with three more gold medals and three more world records, in the 200-meter freestyle, the 100-meter butterfly, and the 4×200-meter freestyle relay. He now had five total, won in just four days, and each of them a world record!

There were still two more events to go, however—and Spitz wasn't so sure he wanted to compete in one of them. So he approached his coach with a request.

"I said, 'Coach, I think it would be better if I scratched from the 100-meter freestyle and saved myself for the 4×100 medley relay. Six gold medals isn't so bad,'" Spitz recalled saying.

Spitz's coach refused to hear of it. Instead, he told Spitz that if he didn't swim the 100-meter freestyle, he'd be cut from the medley relay team! Then he added insult to injury by telling Spitz that people were sure to think he was "chicken" if he pulled out of the 100-meter freestyle.

So Spitz stayed in — and didn't just win the individual race but set his sixth world record. And he wasn't finished yet. In the final event of the men's swimming competition, he swam the butterfly leg of the 4×100-meter medley relay, flashing through the water with such power that his team overtook the leaders to win by four seconds. Their gold medal–winning time, 3:48.16, was another world record.

With that win, Spitz launched himself into Olympic history as the owner of more gold medals earned in a single Olympics than any other athlete. With the two he'd won in 1968, he had a total of nine. Only three other Olympians — Carl Lewis, Larisa Latynina, and Paavo Nurmi — had as many.

But before Spitz had a chance to celebrate, tragic events unfolded in the Olympic Village. In the early morning hours of September 5, Palestinian terrorists broke into the compound, killed an Israeli wrestler and his coach, and took nine other Israeli athletes hostage. They announced that they would assassinate the captives by noon if their demands, which included the release of Arab prisoners being held in an Israeli jail and safe passage to the airport, weren't met.

When negotiations failed, the German authorities

did indeed transport the Palestinians to the airport via helicopter with the hostages. There, they had sharpshooters lying in wait to take out the terrorists.

But their plan went horrifyingly wrong. The Palestinians quickly realized they had walked into a trap. They shot and killed some of the hostages and killed the others by launching a grenade into the helicopter. The terrorists suffered casualties, too, when five of their own were gunned down. A German police officer was also killed. In all, seventeen people lost their lives.

The IOC suspended the Games the next day and held a memorial service to honor the fallen athletes. Then IOC president Avery Brundage made an announcement. "The Games must go on!" he declared.

The competitions did indeed continue, but at least one athlete chose to depart before they were over. Like the Israeli hostages, Mark Spitz was Jewish. When the German government advised him to leave the country for his own safety, he listened.

Several stellar swimmers from the United States followed in Spitz's Olympic wake. In 1984, Ambrose "Rowdy" Gaines scored three gold medals in freestyle events despite being the underdog. One of these medals, for the 4×100-meter relay, was shared by teammate Matt Biondi. Biondi returned to two more Olympic Games and increased his gold medal total to eight. He also earned two silvers and a bronze. One of those silvers might very well have been a gold if not for his blunder.

In 1988, Biondi was the favorite to win the 100-meter butterfly. He had a strong start off the block and was the first to make his turn for the second pool length. He was still in the lead as he neared the finish. Then he made a decision that cost him the win. Instead of powering forward with a final, full stroke, he used just his legs and glided to the wall.

That glide was just too slow. The gold went to Anthony Nesty, a swimmer from the tiny South American country Suriname, who stroked hard all the way to the wall to win with a world-record time of 53.00 seconds. Biondi's time? 53.01.

"Maybe if I had grown my fingernails a little bit longer or kicked a little harder, I would have won," Biondi later commented.

Americans continued to earn medals in swimming events after Biondi. By the end of the 2008 Games in Beijing, they had thirty-one medals, twelve of which were gold. Unbelievably, one swimmer contributed eight of those gold medals: Michael Phelps.

⭐ CHAPTER ELEVEN ⭐

The Greatest Olympic Athlete in History (So Far!)

Michael Phelps was just fifteen years old when he raced at the 2000 Sydney Olympics. He didn't win a medal at those Games, for that year the lanes were ruled by the host city's Ian "the Thorpedo" Thorpe, who swam to three gold medals and two silvers. In 2001, however, Phelps turned heads when he broke the world record in the 200-meter butterfly—twice—the youngest male swimmer to set a world record.

By the time the 2004 Games in Athens rolled around, the nineteen-year-old was being hailed as the top contender in several races. As for Phelps himself, "I'd be excited with one gold medal," he told reporters before his first race, the 400-meter individual medley. "How many people in the world have one Olympic gold medal? That's my goal, and that's going to stay my goal until I accomplish it."

As it turned out, he was ready for a new goal when the race was done. He won easily, with a world-record-setting time of 4:08.26. That was more than three seconds ahead of the silver medalist, Erik Vendt!

His next event was the 4×100-meter freestyle relay. Phelps swam the second leg after lead Ian Crocker. Unfortunately, Crocker, who was reportedly ill, swam sluggishly. While his teammates did their best to make up for the slow start, they ended up with a bronze rather than the gold they'd hoped for.

"We're disappointed," Phelps admitted, "but we're fortunate to get a medal."

The following day, the media lined up to capture the action of the most hotly anticipated race of the Olympic swim program: the 200-meter freestyle. Dubbed the Race of the Century, it pitted Phelps against the event's world-record holder, Ian Thorpe, and the defending Olympic champion, Pieter van den Hoogenband, plus five other swimmers.

One commentator, Olympic swimmer Dara Torres, predicted that the winner of the race would be the one who got off to the fastest start. Her prediction came true. Phelps had a less-than-stellar start, diving almost sideways off the block. While he pushed hard to make up lost ground, he wound up finishing in third behind Thorpe, the winner, and van den Hoogenband. Phelps set a different record; with a time of 1:45.32, he was now the fastest American swimmer in the history of the event.

Still, he was critical of his performance. "I found out I was good," Phelps later wrote, "but not good enough. I had work to do."

Phelps had now won medals in three out of three races. He had five more to go. Unbelievably, when all five were through, he had five more shiny gold medals around his neck! His single Olympic total was six golds and two bronzes. Had he won just one more gold, he would have tied Mark Spitz's long-held record of seven. Had both his bronzes been golds instead, he would have beaten it.

Eight gold medals in one Olympics? It seemed an impossible quest, at least to Ian Thorpe. "I don't think he will do it," said the Australian, who had retired in 2006, "but I'd love to see it."

When Phelps read that reply, he decided to do everything he could to give Thorpe something he'd "love to see."

He started out strong at the 2008 Beijing Games by breaking his own world record in the 400-meter individual medley with an incredible time of 4:03.84.

The next race, the 4×100-meter freestyle relay, was equally dramatic, except this time Phelps was outside the pool cheering the team's anchor, Jason Lezak, on to the finish. Phelps had swum the first leg; now teammate Lezak was a fraction behind the French anchor, Alain Bernard. But at the last moment, he surged ahead to touch the wall first.

"It was epic," Phelps said of Lezak's phenomenal, come-from-behind effort.

One night later, Phelps dove into the pool for the 200-meter freestyle race—and once again broke his own world record by shaving almost a whole second off his time. He added two more world-record wins the next evening, for the 200-meter butterfly and the 4×200-meter freestyle relay.

Five races in four days, all gold medals, all world records. Phelps wasn't just phenomenal, he was unstoppable. Certainly no one was able to stop him in the 200-meter individual medley where he set his sixth world record and took his sixth gold medal in the Games.

He was nearly caught in the 100-meter butterfly, however. That race, his seventh of the Games, proved to be his most challenging. He swam as he always did, going at top speed but saving himself for a spurt of power at the end. With ten meters left, he made his move. Stroking with amazing strength, he drew even with the leader, Serbian swimmer Milorad Cavic—and then lunged ahead, crashing full-force into the wall.

But had he won? He wasn't sure until he took off his goggles and checked the scoreboard. When his name appeared in the top slot, the typically reserved swimmer yelled and slapped the water in triumph. He had just tied Mark Spitz's seemingly unmatchable 1972 achievement of seven gold medals in one Olympic Games!

Phelps never minded the comparison to Spitz, but he never wanted to be the second Mark Spitz. Instead, he wanted to be "the first Michael Phelps...to do something no one had ever done before."

If he was to do that something, he and his teammates had to win their last race: the 4×100-meter medley relay. Going into the race, however, Phelps's coach, Bob Bowman, wasn't one hundred percent sure his team could beat their chief rivals, the Australians. In fact, "Bob told my mom before the race that he thought our chances of winning were 60–40, maybe 70–30," Phelps later recalled.

The race took place on Sunday, August 17. Aaron Peirsol swam the first leg, the backstroke. When the buzzer sounded, he launched backward off the block, dolphin-kicked underwater, and then surfaced and began windmilling his arms furiously. He touched the wall in first place, and Brendan Hansen took off for his breaststroke lap.

Unfortunately Hansen wasn't as strong as his competition. When he hit the wall, the team was in third place.

Then it was Phelps's turn. When he was certain Hansen had touched, he plunged off the block over Hansen and into the water for his butterfly lap. And then—

"I gave it everything I had. Everything," Phelps later wrote. "I drove so hard that my finish was ugly."

Ugly, perhaps, but so powerful, too, that he had reclaimed first place for the team when he finished his lap. Jason Lezak dove in and Phelps, his final Olympic swim done, climbed out to join the frenzied crowd in cheering his teammate on.

It was close, very close, but in the end, Lezak's fingertips brushed the wall before anyone else's did. Thanks to team effort, Michael Phelps had just won a historic eighth gold medal and helped set yet another world record.

In the stands, his mother burst into tears. Sitting in

front of her was Ian Thorpe. He turned and offered this simple but heartfelt congratulations: "Good job. That was great."

Mark Spitz's reaction was equally gracious. "He is the single greatest Olympic athlete of all time now," he told reporters.

The critical word there, of course, is *now*. For as great as Phelps is, someday there may be another Olympic champion equal to or greater than him. And when that athlete takes to the podium, people the world over will surely rejoice in the triumph.

MATT CHRISTOPHER ®

THE #1 SPORTS SERIES FOR KIDS

Read them all!

- Baseball Flyhawk
- Baseball Turnaround
- The Basket Counts
- Body Check
- Catch That Pass!
- Catcher with a Glass Arm
- Center Court Sting
- Centerfield Ballhawk
- Challenge at Second Base
- The Comeback Challenge
- Comeback of the Home Run Kid
- Cool as Ice
- The Diamond Champs
- Dirt Bike Racer
- Dirt Bike Runaway
- Dive Right In

- Double Play at Short
- Face-Off
- Fairway Phenom
- Football Double Threat
- Football Fugitive
- Football Nightmare
- The Fox Steals Home
- Goalkeeper in Charge
- The Great Quarterback Switch
- Halfback Attack*
- The Hockey Machine
- The Home Run Kid Races On
- Hook Shot Hero
- Hot Shot
- Ice Magic
- Johnny Long Legs

*Previously published as *Crackerjack Halfback*

Karate Kick

The Kid Who Only Hit Homers

Lacrosse Face-Off

Lacrosse Firestorm

Long-Arm Quarterback

Long Shot for Paul

Look Who's Playing First Base

Miracle at the Plate

Mountain Bike Mania

Nothin' But Net

Out at Second

Penalty Shot

Power Pitcher**

QB Blitz

Return of the Home Run Kid

Run for It

Shoot for the Hoop

Skateboard Renegade

Skateboard Tough

Slam Dunk

Snowboard Champ

Snowboard Maverick

Snowboard Showdown

Soccer Duel

Soccer Halfback

Soccer Hero

Soccer Scoop

Stealing Home

The Submarine Pitch

The Team That Couldn't Lose

Tight End

Top Wing

Touchdown for Tommy

Tough to Tackle

Wingman on Ice

All available in paperback from Little, Brown and Company

**Previously published as *Baseball Pals*

Matt Christopher®

Sports Bio Bookshelf

Kobe Bryant

Dale Earnhardt Sr.

Jeff Gordon

Tony Hawk

Dwight Howard

LeBron James

Derek Jeter

Michael Jordan

Peyton and Eli Manning

Shaquille O'Neal

Albert Pujols

Jackie Robinson

Alex Rodriguez

Babe Ruth

Tiger Woods